DATE DUE			

People to Know

Elvis Presley

Music Legend, Movie Star, The King

Connie Plantz

E | **Enslow Publishers, Inc.**
40 Industrial Road   PO Box 38
Box 398   Aldershot
Berkeley Heights, NJ 07922 Hants GU12 6BP
USA   UK

http://www.enslow.com

To my loving family,
Gary, Kristen, and Brandon
for treating me like a queen
while I wrote about The King

Library of Congress Cataloging-in-Publication Data

Plantz, Connie.
    Elvis Presley : music legend, movie star, the king / Connie Plantz.
        p. cm. — (People to know)
    Summary: Examines the life of Elvis Presley, the rock and roll singer, guitarist,
and actor who created a sensation with his unique blend of musical styles,
powerful voice, good looks, and scandalous dancing.
    Includes bibliographical references (p.) and index.
    ISBN 0-7660-2103-3 (hardcover)
    1. Presley, Elvis, 1935–1977—Juvenile literature. 2. Rock musicians—United
States—Biography—Juvenile literature. [1. Presley, Elvis, 1935–1977. 2. Singers.
3. Rock music.] I. Title. II. Series.
    ML3930.P73P52 2004
    782.42166'092—dc22
                                      2003015658
Printed in the United States of America

10 9 8 7 6 5 4 3 2 1

To Our Readers
We have done our best to make sure all Internet Addresses in this book were active and
appropriate when we went to press. However, the author and the publisher have no
control over and assume no liability for the material available on those Internet sites or
on other Web sites they may link to. Any comments or suggestions can be sent by e-mail
to comments@enslow.com or to the address on the back cover.

Illustration Credits: *ALL in the Family II*, mural at Sherrod Library, East
Tennessee State University, Johnson City, by artist Marianne DiNapoli Mylet;
based on a print by Williard Gayheart; for more information, see ETSU's
Center for Appalachian Studies and Services, at <http://cass.etsu.edu/
bluegrass/>, p. 108; AP/Wide World Photos, p. 90; © Corbis, pp. 4, 37, 74;
Brandon Plantz, pp. 7, 10, 18, 29, 52, 65, 106, 111; Brandon Plantz, car
courtesy of Tad Pierson of American Dream Safari in Memphis, Tenn., p. 29;
Elvis images used by permission, Elvis Presley Enterprises, Inc., pp. 12, 23,
41, 44, 49, 59, 63, 67, 81, 82, 83, 92, 100; © Ernest C. Withers, courtesy,
Panopticon Gallery, Waltham, MA, pp. 32, 55; National Archives and Records
Administration, pp. 72, 97; © San Diego Historical Society, p. 87.

Cover Illustration: Elvis image used by permission, Elvis Presley
Enterprises, Inc.

Contents

Elvis Presley

Presley Power

One boy jumped young Elvis Presley from behind, pinning his arms to his sides. Another boy fished Elvis's car keys from his pocket "If you play something, you'll get your car keys back," they taunted.

Elvis picked up his small guitar and muttered, "I'll try but I really don't know that much." Skillfully, he played a snappy tune called "Under the Double Eagle."

"It just blew me away," said Ronny, a classmate from woodshop class who witnessed the incident. "I didn't even know he could play that guitar—I just thought he was fixing it for somebody else."[1]

Only Elvis's closest friends at Humes High School in Memphis, Tennessee, knew that he had musical talent. Elvis once said that the other students thought of him as a "squirrel," a misfit.[2] He did not even try to fit in with the other boys, who wore jeans and T-shirts. Instead, Elvis wore fashionable dress-up clothes. His long hair was styled with a greasy mixture of rose oil tonic and Vaseline petroleum jelly. He grinned a lopsided, sneerlike expression that made him seem as if he had a secret. And he did have at least one: He planned to enter the annual senior talent show.

Elvis had been preparing for this opportunity all his life. His whole social and personal world revolved around music. He had studied a range of musical styles: pop, jazz, country, gospel, hillbilly and blues. Elvis knew them all.

Like Elvis, many Humes High School students had migrated with their families from small rural towns to Memphis, Tennessee, after World War II. Knowing this, Elvis chose to sing a country-and-western song and borrowed a red flannel shirt for his performance. He knew that much of the audience had been raised on country music. Their applause would determine the winner. Elvis planned to win. The prize was a chance to perform a second song.

On April 9, 1953, sixteen hundred people filled the school auditorium. Elvis was the sixteenth of twenty-one acts listed on the program. He paced behind the curtain as a baton twirler, xylophone trio, and accordionist performed. Finally, act fifteen, the school band, finished. The audience glanced at the program. Number sixteen, misspelled, read, "Guitarist . . . Elvis Prestly."[3]

Elvis shyly appeared from behind the curtain.

Elvis's high school (now a middle school) is a famous landmark. Students give tours during Elvis Week every August.

Though he was tall, gangly, and blond, he looked small on the large stage. He stepped up to the microphone carrying his guitar strapped across his shoulder. Rumbling and whispering rolled through the audience.[4]

Elvis stood quiet and somber. His blue eyes canvassed the audience. He sneered. After a minute or two he swung his guitar from his hip to his chest, strummed a chord, and belted out, "Keep Them Cold Icy Fingers Off of Me." This funny song is about a man being chased in his nightmares by skeletons.

Whenever a skeleton gets near the man, he warns, "Keep them cold icy fingers off of me." Each time Elvis repeated the chorus, he held the word "cold" for a second and put a shiver in his voice.

After performing, Elvis retreated behind the curtain to enthusiastic claps and cheers. He waited by himself. Five more acts danced, flipped, and drummed onstage. Finally, Miss Scrivener, the show's organizer, announced the winner: Elvis Presley.

With more confidence, Elvis returned to the stage for his encore. Simply and clearly he sang "Till I Waltz With You Again." His voice conveyed a lover's promise to be faithful until he danced with his girl again. Elvis's low notes resonated like a cat's purr. His high notes brought tears to listeners' eyes. Grown women in the crowd sobbed.[5]

When he stopped singing, the entire audience stood and cheered. Elvis turned to his teacher: "They really liked me, Miss Scrivener. They really liked me."[6]

Elvis had always expected something special to happen to him. After the talent show, his popularity grew. He brought his guitar to school every day and sang ballads to the students who flocked around him. No longer did they call him names or taunt him.

According to Elvis, winning the senior talent show was the beginning of his rise to fame.[7] Winning confirmed his belief that hard work, not luck, led to success. From that day forward, he worked hard to fulfill his dreams of being a movie star and singer.

Tupelo Talent

On January 8, 1935, twenty-two-year-old Gladys Presley sent her husband, Vernon, to fetch the doctor. He drove a mile past cotton fields and cornfields to find Dr. William Hunt in the town of Tupelo, Mississippi. Dr. Hunt arrived at the Presleys' two-room house in time to help Gladys deliver twin boys. By the light of a flickering kerosene lamp, the first twin was delivered. He was stillborn. Thirty-five minutes later, at 4:35 A.M., Elvis Aaron (sometimes spelled Aron) was born. Gladys, near death, was admitted to the hospital charity ward along with Elvis. Eighteen-year-old Vernon Presley had no money to pay the $15 hospital bill for his wife and son.[1]

Gladys Presley believed Elvis received the strength

The Presley house in Tupelo had just two rooms—a bedroom and a kitchen. Today, fans can visit a museum and meditation chapel behind the house. A recording of Elvis singing religious music is played inside the chapel.

of his twin brother, Jessie Garon, who had died. Perhaps this belief gave her hope. She knew Elvis would need to be strong to survive in East Tupelo, Mississippi. His future looked bleak. Education there was a luxury. Hard work was a necessity. To make matters worse, Elvis was born during the Great Depression. Jobs were scarce. Vernon had recently lost his milk delivery job because most people could not afford to buy milk. He did odd jobs around town, such as helping people mend fences or picking crops. However, he did not earn enough to provide for his family. Often, a meal consisted of only cornbread and water.[2]

Fortunately, many relatives lived nearby. They would bring home-grown food and gather on the front porch to sing hymns.

The Presleys' tiny house was in a section of East Tupelo called "above the highway." On these five streets lived the poorest white laborers. Amid rowdy neighbors and crime, Gladys constantly worried about Elvis's safety. She seldom left him, even for a trip to the store.

Gladys Presley's burden of watching over Elvis became even heavier when her husband was sent to prison for forging a check. Vernon had sold a hog to his ex-boss, Orville Bean. Expecting to be paid well, Vernon felt cheated when he saw the small number on the check. He altered Bean's $4 check to a higher amount. Bean pressed criminal charges, and the judge sentenced Vernon Presley to three years at Parchman Farm Prison. Every other Sunday, Elvis and his mother rode the bus for five hours to visit his father.

Gladys Presley tried to support herself and Elvis. She worked at Mid-South Laundry and picked cotton with Elvis riding on her long cloth sack.[3] Still, she did not earn enough money for the house payments. Orville Bean, who owned the property, evicted them. Gladys Presley took her son and moved in with her cousins, Frank and Leona Richards.

Elvis constantly cried for his father.[4] He had nightmares and started walking in his sleep. Attending the First Assembly of God Tabernacle on Sundays cheered him up. The congregation of neighbors, relatives, and a guitar-playing preacher sang joyful

This picture of Elvis with his mother and father may have been taken just before Vernon Presley went to prison.

hymns like "It's a Grand and Glorious Feeling." One time Elvis became so excited by the music that he wiggled off his mother's lap and mimicked the swaying movements of the choir. Sermons about God's love and prayer helped the two endure the time while Vernon was away from the family. Meanwhile, Gladys Presley, friends, and even Orville Bean wrote to the governor of Tennessee, requesting Vernon Presley's release. After nine months, Elvis's father returned home.

Elvis started school in 1941. In the mornings

Gladys Presley, aunts, and cousins walked six-year-old Elvis to the East Tupelo Consolidated School. Dressed in clean hand-me-downs, Elvis learned how to read and write. He was not the best student, but at home he used his new skills to read comic books. Batman, Superman, and Captain Marvel provided him with imaginative adventures.[5]

Vernon Presley stayed in nearby towns to work. He returned home only on weekends. It was on these weekends that Elvis found his freedom. Gladys Presley allowed eight-year-old Elvis to go with his friend James Ausborn to Tupelo every other Saturday morning. They visited WELO radio station, where James's brother, Carvel, had a daily show. His radio name was Mississippi Slim. The boys watched him sing and play his guitar for his show, *Singin' and Pickin' Hillbilly*. Afterward, they would run across the lawn past the statue of a Confederate soldier to the courthouse.

From a large room inside the courthouse, WELO broadcast *The Saturday Jamboree*. This show invited amateurs to come up to the microphone and sing. An audience of local citizens watched and clapped. After waiting in a long line, Elvis sang "Old Shep," a ballad about a boy and his faithful old dog.

These performances boosted Elvis's confidence. In fifth grade, he volunteered to sing during prayer time. His teacher admired the sweetness of his voice. She asked Elvis to sing for the principal. Impressed, the principal chose Elvis as one of the school representatives in the talent contest at the Mississippi-Alabama State Fair.

On October 3, 1945, Children's Day, students from all over the region filed into the huge grandstand at the state fair to witness the talent competition. Elvis sang "Old Shep" without any musical accompaniment. A girl from his school won first prize. Elvis came in fifth. Still, he and the girl remained friends and sang duets at school assemblies.[6]

As World War II ended, Vernon used his savings to buy a brand-new house from Orville Bean for $2,000. He made a $200 down payment. Settled in this four-room house, the Presleys became more active in their church. Elvis taught himself how to play the church piano. He and his parents formed a singing group and entertained at church revivals and conventions.

Five months later, for Elvis's eleventh birthday, his mother bought him his first real guitar. His old one had been so small that relatives always teased him. They joked that Elvis must have gotten it free by collecting bubble-gum wrappers and sending them in for a prize.[7] Elvis was proud of his new guitar. He asked relatives and Mississippi Slim to help him learn chords and techniques.

After a year, Vernon lost his job, and the Presleys moved from East Tupelo to Tupelo. They rented a small shack on Mulberry Alley. This was next to the African-American section of town, called Shake Rag. To Elvis, music had no barriers or color. He attended the revival gospel meetings held at the African-American church down the street from his home.

Elvis's new school, Milam, had only white students. African-American children had to attend a separate school because Tupelo was a segregated town. Blacks and whites did not go to the same schools or churches. They did not sit together on buses or at ball games. At Milam, Elvis felt the prejudice of the more affluent city students. They grouped together dressed in new jeans, sweaters, and leather shoes. Elvis and the poorer rural students were shunned because they wore overalls and went barefoot. Elvis did not let their unkind treatment intimidate him and keep him from entering the school talent show. Although he lost, his music helped him make friends. He played his guitar at school every day, until some eighth-grade boys cut the strings. Missing his music, other students collected money and bought him new ones.[8]

In January 1948, Vernon Presley bought his family a Philco Radio Phonograph so they could listen to the radio or to recordings of their favorite music.[9] In the days before tapes and CDs, music was played on records. Small records had one song on each side of the record. Albums had several songs per side.

The Philco Radio Phonograph was an expensive purchase, and in the following months Vernon Presley had to borrow money to pay his bills. In November he decided to move his family to Memphis, Tennessee, where he hoped to find a good job. Elvis's classmates begged him to sing one last song before leaving. Elvis sang a folk song titled "The Leaves on the Tree."[10]

The Presleys tied their few belongings to the top of their 1937 Plymouth. As they passed the woods of Tupelo, they left behind their friends but not their music and memories. They knew the phonograph and Elvis's guitar would brighten dark lonely nights.

3

Memphis Music

The Presleys settled into one room of a north Memphis boardinghouse. Sixty people lived in the four-story Victorian house. Gladys immediately started scrubbing the filthy room.

Elvis entered Humes High School. On the first day, he came home early, complaining that the school was too big. Gladys escorted him for the next few weeks to be sure he stayed all day.

During Elvis's first year, he blended in with the other students. The following year, teachers began to notice him. His English teacher thought his English was atrocious. His music teacher refused to let him join the glee club, saying "he couldn't sing."[1] Elvis did not dispute the English teacher's claim, but music was another story. He insisted he could sing. To convince the teacher, he brought his guitar and sang "Keep Them Cold Icy Fingers Off of Me." She was not impressed. On his report card she gave him a C. One classmate later observed that the music teacher "didn't appreciate his kind of singing."[2]

Having few friends, Elvis spent his time with relatives. After school he would visit with his cousin Gene Smith. Gene worked at Hall's Grocery Store. Elvis and Gene would sit at the snack bar in the store and drink purple cows. As they sipped the mixture of grape soda and vanilla ice cream, they would talk about their lives and their futures.[3] Elvis spoke of making enough money to buy a home for his mother.

Gladys Presley wanted a new home. She worked as a part-time seamstress, and Vernon Presley worked at United Paint. Still, they could not afford to move. In order to get a better place for a reduced rent, Gladys applied to the Memphis Housing Authority for government help. As a result, the Presleys moved in the fall of 1949 to a redbrick apartment complex called Lauderdale Courts.

For the first time in their lives, the Presleys enjoyed running water, electricity, a bathtub, two bedrooms, and a kitchen. In addition, the apartment complex of 433 units felt like a small community. The residents' lives intertwined as their children played together under magnolia trees on an open grassy area called the Market Mall.[4]

Elvis became friends with neighbors Farley Guy, Paul Dougher, and Buzzy Forbess. They started a football team and challenged other teams from Lauderdale Courts. The three friends hosted parties

Today these apartments are in disrepair, but when the Presleys lived in Lauderdale Courts, it was a thriving, friendly community. Elvis and his parents lived in a first-floor apartment.

in the basement, charging twenty-five cents for sodas and popcorn. Girls came stylishly dressed in pleated skirts, sweaters, black patent-leather shoes, and socks. At the parties, Elvis did not dance. Instead, he stood by the record player, swaying to the slow tunes like "Harbor Lights" and tapping his feet to the new hits, such as "Rudolph the Red-Nosed Reindeer" recorded by country singer Gene Autry.

On Elvis's fifteenth birthday, his father gave him a paperback book of cartoons. He inscribed the book, "May your birthday be sprinkled through and through with joy and love and good times too."[5]

At Lauderdale Courts, Elvis did have a good time. Music was everywhere. Residents played accordions, fiddles, guitars, and horns. Elvis jammed with them in the grassy area. At other times he followed the older boys as they paraded through the complex holding their guitars. They were professionals who played in groups around town.

One of these musicians taught Elvis how to play a fast tune called "That's All Right (Mama)." The two repeated it so many times that a man tossed a bucket of water on their heads from his upstairs apartment.[6] This song had been sung and written by an African-American singer named Arthur "Big Boy" Crudup. Although African Americans were banned from the white residential areas, their music permeated the complex and much of the rest of Memphis.

Many residents listened to B. B. King, a blues guitarist who was also a disc jockey on the African-American radio station. He played his own music as well as records of other African-American artists. Also on this station was Reverend Brewster. He invited whites to come to his church and hear the music. Elvis often accepted the invitation, sitting in the separate section for white people.

Elvis looked forward to the monthly all-night gospel sings. He would go with his parents and his cousin Gene to the Ellis Auditorium in Memphis. Elvis enjoyed the showmanship of the experienced entertainers. He was fascinated by the outlandish antics of the bass player in the Statesmen, a singing group. Big Chief jiggled his legs till the preacher told him to stop. The group's song "If the Lord Wasn't

Walking by My Side" sent Elvis and the audience into a frenzy of snapping fingers, shouting "Amen," and swaying arms.

Elvis longed to be on that stage, and he took steps to get there. He struggled through guitar lessons from the preacher's son, who played professionally. When neighbors complained about Elvis's constant playing and singing, he retreated to the laundry room to practice.[7]

Once Elvis mastered a song, he would go into a variety store on Main Street called W. T. Grant. There, in a private recording booth, he would drop a quarter into a machine and sing. The machine recorded his voice on a flimsy plastic record. At home he would listen to the record on his phonograph.

To make money, Elvis got a part-time job as an usher at a movie theater in Memphis. Dressed in a uniform, he helped moviegoers find seats, then relaxed and watched the movies. He liked to study the male actors portraying tough guys in black leather jackets. In *Rebel Without a Cause*, movie star James Dean acted sullen and brooded a lot. Elvis decided to imitate Dean by smiling less. "You can't be a rebel if you grin," he said.[8]

His earnings paid for a television set for his parents. Situation comedies like *I Love Lucy* and variety shows entertained the family. News reports of possible nuclear war with Russia gave the Presleys more to worry about.

Elvis preferred the radio to the television. Radio disc jockeys joked and talked. They reached out to the teen audience. Elvis listened to all the newest tunes and learned new singing styles. Johnny Ray in his number-one hit "Cry" dramatized his words. He communicated with his voice. Elvis had never heard anything like this before. He also heard songs by black singers on a white Cincinnati, Ohio, station. The disc jockey was taking a risk playing this music. He waited until late at night after his classical music show was over.

At school, Elvis joined the Reserve Officers' Training Corp (ROTC). He wore a uniform, marched, and saluted while learning military basics from an army officer. He also played on the junior football team until the coach found fault with his hair and ordered him to cut it. When Elvis did not comply, some players attacked him in the restroom. Red West, a football star, came along in the nick of time and stopped the beating.

After school, Elvis and his friends visited Beale Street, the main street of the Memphis African-American community. There they heard the sound of rhythm-and-blues music coming from the bars. Another opportunity to hear African-American artists was in a district called Orange Mound. In a special late-night show, whites watched African-American entertainers Dizzy Gillespie, Bobby Blue Bland, and Little Junior Parker.[9]

Elvis admired the entertainers' attire so much that he started imitating their flamboyant clothing style. He took clothes from a church donation box at the Poplar Street Mission.[10] He also bought clothes on credit at Lansky's tailor shop at the end of Beale Street. A pink shirt, a black bolero jacket, and a pair of dress pants with a side stripe was Elvis's favorite attire for school. To hide his long neck, he would turn his shirt collar up. At one football game, he strutted around the track with sunglasses, a sport coat, and an ascot—a neck scarf.

Elvis grew bushy sideburns to imitate the tough truckers he saw driving through Memphis. Once he curled his hair with a home permanent and dyed it with black shoe polish to resemble Tony Curtis, his favorite movie star. Shoe polish does not make a good hair dye: When Elvis had to push his father's stalled 1941 Lincoln in the rain, the shoe polish dripped onto his face.[11]

By Elvis's eighteenth birthday, the other Humes students were noticing his unique style. It was not until four months later, at the senior talent show, that they recognized his talent. After Elvis won the encore, the yearbook editors mentioned Elvis twice in the pages of the 1953 Humes High *Herald*. First, they said he was a teacher's pet because teachers always cried when he sang. Second, they predicted Elvis Presley's future would be playing hillbilly music at the local bar.[12]

Elvis ended his senior year by taking Regis Vaughan to the prom. He had been dating fourteen-year-old Regis for three months. Dressed in a rented blue tuxedo, Elvis escorted Regis, who wore a strapless formal, to the Peabody Hotel. Because Elvis could not dance, they talked while hit songs such as "Rock Around the Clock" played in the background.

In June 1953, Elvis appeared on the Ellis Auditorium stage, where his proud parents watched him

Throughout his life, Elvis enjoyed playing football.

receive a high-school diploma. Vernon and Gladys Presley, who had not completed elementary school, breathed a sigh of relief. They believed Elvis's diploma would help him get a good steady job. Elvis, too, was relieved. Throughout his high school years, he had daydreamed about being a movie star and a singer. Now he was free to pursue his dreams.

Sun Sound

On July 1, 1953, Elvis started a job in a factory refurbishing flame-throwers, a World War II weapon. Working five days a week, eight hours a day, he earned $33, which was a typical weekly salary at the time for an educated person in the South. After he had been working for two weeks, an article appeared in the *Memphis Press-Scimitar* about Sam Phillips, who owned Sun Records and the Memphis Recording Service. The article focused on Sun's newest hit record, "Just Walkin' in the Rain" by the Prisonaires. The band members were actual inmates at a prison. Phillips had liked this group so much that he arranged for them to come with guards to record their music at his studio. The article also said that Phillips was searching for different types of music.

Elvis really wanted to make music, not weapons. On a hot, humid Saturday at the end of July, he took a step toward making his dreams a reality. Elvis walked up to the small redbrick building on Union Street in Memphis. As he opened the door, Marion Keisker stopped typing and glanced up.

Keisker saw a boy with greased black hair and sideburns carrying a beat-up guitar. She thought he was a drifter looking for a handout.[1] Elvis told her he wanted to make a record and lied that it was for his mother's birthday. Then he added, "If you know anyone that needs a singer . . . "

"What kind of a singer are you?" asked Keisker.

"I sing all kinds," answered Elvis.

"Who do you sound like?"

"I don't sound like nobody."

"Hillbilly?"

"I sing hillbilly," said Elvis.

"Who do you sound like in hillbilly?"

"I don't sound like nobody," said Elvis.[2]

Elvis followed Marion Keisker through the door behind her desk into a green acoustic-tiled recording studio. Piles of records filled the corners of the room, and in the middle stood a microphone. Keisker left Elvis and went into the recording booth, which contained a single-track recording machine.

When she signaled, Elvis strummed simple chords on his guitar. His voice flowed in an emotional ebb from low to high. His slow tune, "My Happiness," was carefully sung and filled with emotion. Then he picked up the beat and added a bluesy feel.

Elvis, aware that Sam Phillips recorded African-American singers, next sang "That's When Your Heartaches Begin." It was a song made popular by the Ink Spots, an African-American group. The tune warns about the sorrow of finding your girl in a friend's arms. Elvis imitated the Ink Spots' sound and dialect. He even finished the song like the Ink Spots' lead singer, who spoke the words with a deep voice and fake accent.

Having heard many amateurs, Marion Keisker knew Elvis's sound was unique. She recognized his ability to sing with soul.[3] "Soul" was a term usually used to describe the deep emotional quality of African-American vocalists.

She made an extra recording of Elvis's singing for Sam Phillips to hear when he returned to the studio. Keisker and Phillips, who were experienced in the music business, believed music was on the verge of changing. The big dance bands of the 1930s and 1940s had almost disappeared. Modern pop singers seemed stodgy. They did not appeal to the teenagers. Country music, popular in the South, remained traditional. Up North, the radio stations played and sold music sung by African-American singers. Teens loved the beat and lyrics of their music. Phillips was looking for an artist to sing with that same style and soul—but, for the racist Southerners, that artist had to be white.

Elvis's slow songs did not reveal whether he had what Phillips was looking for, but Marion Keisker knew he was worth hearing again. Her feeling was confirmed when a woman in the waiting room said that Elvis's voice gave her goose bumps. Meanwhile, Elvis thought he had failed: "My guitar sounded like someone beating on a bucket lid."[4]

During the fall of 1953, Elvis lived a double life. During the day, he drove a truck for Crown Electric. At night, he entertained in small clubs. Regularly, he stopped at Sun Records and the Memphis Recording Service to ask Keisker if she knew of any group looking for a singer.

Three months later, Sam Phillips started recording country-and-western music. Elvis felt this might be his chance. He paid Keisker his $4 to cut a record. Elvis was pleased to see that Sam Phillips was there. The two country songs that Elvis sang gave Phillips a good idea of his voice. It was simple, clear, and practiced. Nothing unique. The only originality in the songs was when Elvis stopped the monotonous strumming of his guitar and played a little stronger. Phillips was indifferent but said he might call Elvis back.

While waiting for that call, Elvis continued to find music around Memphis. He started regularly attending the Assembly of God Church in South Memphis. The church had a hundred-voice choir. Plus, the Blackwood Brothers, a famous quartet, performed there.

In a church Bible study class, Elvis met Dixie Locke. She was a senior at Southside High School. Dixie liked the fact that Elvis was different.[5] On dates, they listened to records and attended all-night gospel

Elvis recorded his first songs in this building. Each recording was pressed onto two sides of a plastic disk.

sings. Saturday afternoons were spent at the Memphis radio station WMPS. The couple sat in the front row and watched disc jockey Bob Neal's *High Noon Roundup Radio Show* through a huge glass window. Neal's guests sang and played country and gospel music.

Elvis and Dixie would go to the movie theater and listen to music at Charlie's Record Shop. The shop had hundreds of records. Dixie and Elvis heard new and old hits as they sat inside a listening booth.

Sometimes Elvis played "My Happiness," the record that he had made at Sun Records. In the evenings, the couple would park at K's Drive-In for cheeseburgers and milkshakes. Waitresses delivered their food to the car on a tray.

Most of the local artists sang with a group. Elvis wanted to be a lead singer. He auditioned for two groups and was rejected by both. One said his voice did not blend with theirs. The other group leader told Elvis to stick to truck driving because he could not sing.

Elvis did not give up. He became a one-man show. He would walk around Memphis with his guitar slung over his shoulder, searching for an audience. Firefighters sitting at the station and café customers listened to Elvis play his combination of rock and country music.

On Saturday, June 26, 1954, six months after Elvis Presley had last visited Sun Records, Phillips needed a singer to record a new song. Marion Keisker suggested the kid with the sideburns. Sam could not remember the name of the shy boy. Keisker found the tape she had made a year ago. She called the phone number she had written on the tape.

Elvis was so excited when he heard her voice. He rushed to the studio. "I was there by the time she hung up the phone," he exaggerated.[6] At Sun, Elvis worked all afternoon to meet Phillips's expectations of how the song should sound. He could not do it. Still, Sam Phillips recognized that Elvis's singing had potential. He asked Elvis to sing songs he knew. For three hours Elvis sang pop songs, spirituals, anything he could think of.[7]

Phillips called Scotty Moore, a professional musician, to work with Elvis. Moore, twenty-one, led a group called the Starlite Wranglers, which had recently made a record at Sun Records. Scotty agreed to help Elvis. Bill Black, who lived nearby, added his bass playing to the practice session.

On July 5, 1954, the trio went to the Sun Records studio. Again, Elvis tried in vain. Phillips left the room. Feeling more relaxed, Elvis remembered the song he had sung at Lauderdale Courts called "That's All Right (Mama)." He plucked his guitar strings and foolishly jumped around the studio. His uninhibited raw voice drew out the word "mama," and he replaced lyrics with "ah dee dee dee dee," just as illiterate singers in Tupelo did when they could not read the words. Scotty Moore and Bill Black jumped into the fun with the electric guitar and bass.

Phillips, standing in the hallway, could not believe his ears. He had never heard music like this before. It had a great dance beat. Phillips persuaded his friend to play Elvis's song on the radio. Dewy Phillips, a white disc jockey, usually played African-American music on his show, *Red Hot and Blue.* He agreed to play Elvis's song because he sounded African-American.

The night it was going to be played, Elvis could not stand the suspense. He worried that friends would laugh at him. Not bearing to listen to it himself, he went to the movie theater. But before leaving home, he turned on the radio, set the station, and instructed his parents not to touch the dial.

When Elvis was growing up, strict segregation laws ruled the South. White people and black people did not mix at school, at work, or at play. African Americans could not visit this Memphis zoo except on the days set aside for them.

Dewy Phillips played "That's All Right (Mama)" on his show. Before the record was over, forty-seven listeners called to ask the singer's name. They requested the song be continuously replayed. Fourteen times in a row, Phillips played Elvis's "That's All Right (Mama)."

Gladys and Vernon Presley sat shocked beside the radio until the phone rang. Dewy Phillips wanted Elvis to come quickly to the radio station to be interviewed on the air.

Elvis's parents searched the dark movie theater until they found Elvis. When his mother told him to go to the radio station, Elvis began shaking all over. At the station, Dewy Phillips interviewed Elvis without telling him that the microphone was on. He asked Elvis the name of the high school he had attended. "Humes," mumbled Elvis. The listeners knew that Humes was an all-white school. They realized that although his singing style sounded African-American, Elvis was white. White teens were ecstatic. Finally, they had a singer who produced great dance music. They had not been allowed to buy African-American singers' music because of racism—but they would be allowed to buy an Elvis Presley record.

After this glorious night, Elvis, Bill Black, and Scotty Moore spent four evenings working on different songs for the flip side of the record. Playing around, Bill Black started singing "Blue Moon of Kentucky," a popular country song. Elvis copied him, speeding up the beat and giving it his bluesy touch. Sam added an echo effect called slapback. Moore and Black kept the beat going and going to create another hit.

Elvis did with notes and rhythm what painters do with colors. He mixed and blended black rhythm and blues with hillbilly music, creating a new sound called rockabilly. From that moment, traditional country music slipped in popularity. Rockabilly became the new music of the South. Sun Records received orders for five thousand records of "That's All Right (Mama)"/"Blue Moon of Kentucky" before the records were even made.[8] Elvis Presley was on his way to becoming the "King of Western Bop."[9]

Rockabilly Rebel

Elvis proudly watched his record come off the press at Buster William's Plastic Products in Memphis.[1] Elvis Presley, Scotty Moore, and Bill Black had decided to call their group Hillbilly Cat and the Blue Moon Boys.[2] It was a name that identified their music. "Cat music" was another term for rhythm and blues.

The group's first public performance was at the Bon Air Club in Memphis. The audience did not appreciate the musical mixture. They stared at Elvis in bewilderment while he sang his two new hits. After the performance, Elvis told Sam Phillips, "I just feel like . . . I failed."[3]

Phillips was not worried. He had been in the music business long enough to recognize a star. He quickly got Elvis in front of the public again by adding him to a show scheduled at Overton Park Shell, an outdoor theater in Memphis.

Dixie drove Elvis to the performance. All the way he nervously drummed his fingers on the dashboard. He became agitated when he discovered that Sam Phillips was late. Finally Phillips arrived and assured Elvis he would do well.

The discussion was interrupted by the announcer presenting "*Elvin* Presley." Elvis repeated his act from the high school talent show. First, he glared at the audience sitting in tiers of wooden seats. Next, he leaned into the mike and sneered his crooked smile. Finally, he strummed the guitar and blasted "That's All Right (Mama)." His voice had the same deep, simple, bluesy rock tone of the recording. He shook one leg then the other to the beat of the music. His baggy pants exaggerated each movement until they appeared to take on a life of their own. The crowd went wild. Elvis thought they were making fun of him until they shouted, "Encore!" He obliged by wiggling his legs more as he sang "Blue Moon Over Kentucky."

Elvis Presley became well known in Memphis. Sam Phillips wanted people in other towns to hear Elvis's records and buy them. To accomplish this, Phillips personally took the records to individual radio stations.

As Phillips traveled throughout the South, he found the record was not an easy sell. Most disc jockeys refused to play it because it did not fit into the music style they played. Each station had a specialty, and Elvis's new musical concoction did not fit into any

Sam Phillips, left, of Sun Records knew that Elvis was going to be a big star. He signed a contract with Elvis to make four records. Each small record held two songs—one on each side.

category. No one knew if it was country, popular, or rhythm and blues. Even Elvis's hometown station, WELO in Tupelo, refused to broadcast it because Elvis's style sounded too much like a type of music, called "race" music, that was sung by African Americans performers. WELO only played records sung by white singers who sounded white. Ironically, a station that played only African-American music agreed to play Elvis's music.

Elvis also marketed his record. He played "That's All Right (Mama)" on the jukeboxes at record stores and the roller rink. He played it over and over again.

Every morning Elvis would go to his job at Crown Electric. He saved his $40-a-week earnings to buy a 1942 Martin D-18 guitar for $175. He paid extra to have his name spelled in metal letters on the body of the guitar below the strings. The store owner did not think much of Elvis's old guitar. He gave Elvis $8 for it, then dropped it into the trash. "Shucks it still played good," complained Elvis.[4]

On August 26, 1954, Elvis Presley signed a contract with Sun Records. He agreed to record at least four records, eight sides. Still, getting Elvis to record seriously was a difficult task. At the recording sessions, the nineteen-year-old goofed around. Never ready, he would improvise while trying to find the right rhythm and sound of a song. It was a long, tedious process. Sam Phillips tolerated Elvis's silliness because he believed the more fun a singer had, the better his work would be.[5]

Elvis did not let him down. On his second record, "I Don't Care If the Sun Don't Shine," Moore and Black played bouncing carousel music. Elvis added a rock 'n' roll beat. His voice rose and fell with high and low notes. "Good Rockin' Tonight," the flip side, was perfect for Elvis's rockabilly style and the steady backbeat of the electric guitar and bass.

"Blue Moon Over Kentucky" reached number three on the country-and-western charts of best-selling records. Because of this success, Sam Phillips talked a friend into letting Elvis perform on a country radio show called the Grand Ole Opry. Elvis was honored. Since 1925, the show had been very popular. Country stars usually spent years trying to get their big chance to perform on this Nashville, Tennessee, stage.

Elvis rented a tuxedo and dressed in the restroom of a nearby service station because the Ryman Auditorium had no dressing rooms. Backstage, Elvis's fear of not pleasing the audience haunted him.

This time, his fears were justified. Elvis's rockabilly version of "Blue Moon Over Kentucky" left the audience clapping politely. Backstage, the show's talent agent told Elvis to forget singing and continue driving his truck.

Elvis cried all the way home. It took him weeks to get over it.[6]

His next big opportunity was the Louisiana Hayride radio show. Second to the Grand Ole Opry in popularity, it had a younger audience. The show was broadcast live on Saturday nights from Shreveport, Louisiana. Elvis performed twice on October 16, 1954. The early show did not go well. The middle-aged audience was perplexed by his style.

Elvis found the perfect audience for his music at the later show. College students screamed and cheered so loud, Elvis could not hear himself sing. Afterward, they rushed the stage and took his picture. The producers of the Louisiana Hayride saw that Elvis could attract new young listeners. They hired the Hillbilly Cat and the Blue Moon Boys to play every Saturday. Elvis would be paid $18 dollars a show as the lead singer. Scotty Moore and Bill Black would earn $12 each.

When "Good Rockin' Tonight" reached number three on the regional charts, Elvis quit his job at

Crown Electric. Vernon Presley disapproved. He believed Elvis could make more money staying with the company and becoming an electrician.[7]

Elvis was determined to become famous. Traveling in Scotty Moore's 1954 Chevy, the trio toured the South. Anywhere people were willing to pay, the group performed. Their audiences ranged from picnickers at small park gatherings to students packed into high school auditoriums. Regardless of the crowd, they performed their best. As a result, Elvis would enter a town unknown and exit a star.[8]

Despite his busy schedule, Elvis always called home to reassure his mother he was safe. During the week, Presley, Moore, and Black went farther and farther from Memphis. On two-lane highways, they drove as far west as Roswell, New Mexico, north to St. Louis, Missouri, east to Norfolk, Virginia, and south to Fort Myers, Florida. No matter what their location, they had to return to Shreveport, Louisiana, for the Hayride program on Saturday nights. In sixteen months they played more than two hundred dates and covered one hundred thousand miles.

Elvis's sense of humor, pranks, and practical jokes kept the weary travelers alert. They could not keep him still. He chewed his fingernails, tapped, drummed, and combed his hair. Additionally, Elvis insisted they stop at every fireworks stand to buy firecrackers. Scotty Moore and Bill Black resorted to pillow fights and wrestling with Elvis to wear him out.

Back at Sun Records they recorded "Milk Cow Blues." In this song, Elvis teased the listener. First he sang slow. Next he ordered the musicians, "Let's get

Hillbilly Cat and the Blue Moon Boys: When Elvis sang, it was as if someone turned on a switch. Bill Black on bass and Scotty Moore on guitar kept up the beat.

real gone for a change." They played faster. Elvis sang to a rock 'n' roll beat. The flip side was the country tune "You're a Heartbreaker." Elvis sped it up while keeping the original tune and feel. Sam Phillips always put two types of music on a record. This way, the record would be played on two types of specialty radio stations.

Back home, Elvis ended a spectacular year by buying his first car. It was a used tan 1951 Lincoln Cosmopolitan. He had "Elvis Presley–Sun Records" painted on the side. He started traveling separately from Bill Black and Scotty Moore. His band mates were tired of being mobbed by fans everywhere they went. Since Elvis never liked to be alone, he recruited other friends to travel with him. Red West, who had saved Elvis from getting beat up in the high school restroom, and Elvis's cousin Gene Smith were his first companions.

Before they left on tour, Elvis made his fourth single. He added a rock backbeat to an old song called "Baby Let's Play House." For this number, Elvis used a new vocal technique. He hiccuped and stuttered while singing the lyrics.

On January 15, 1955, Elvis appeared on the Louisiana Hayride stage wearing a rust-colored suit, black-dotted purple tie, and pink socks. In the audience sat Colonel Tom Parker, who ran a company called Jamboree Attractions. One of his clients was Hank Snow, a famous country-and-western star. Parker managed Hank Snow and a group of entertainers who traveled around the country. Parker saw the audience's enthusiastic reaction to the handsome young man on the stage. He invited Elvis and his musicians to join the Hank Snow tour.

Elvis's first performance as part of this group was at the Dallas, Texas, "D" Jamboree. Adults paid sixty cents and children paid thirty cents to attend. Most important, the performance was transmitted live on a radio show that reached across Texas.

Being part of the Hank Snow Jamboree spread Elvis's fame. Texans especially liked Elvis. He dressed in a pink sport coat with big black fabric teardrops on the front, pink shirt, and black pants with a pink side stripe. He strummed the guitar strings so hard they snapped. Because of his wild movements, Texans nicknamed him "Elvis the Pelvis." A sellout concert in Houston, Texas, turned away two thousand people. Five thousand fans came to his Waco, Texas, performance.

Elvis received so much attention that headlining country singers refused to perform with him. At a show in Orlando, Florida, Hank Snow performed after Elvis's act. The audience hollered, "Bring Elvis back!" The announcer, embarrassed for Snow, informed the crowd Elvis could not return because he was out back signing autographs. Frantically, the audience rushed out to get an autograph, leaving Hank Snow standing on the stage. Elvis had upstaged one of the most famous singers in country music.

Two days later, in Jacksonville, Florida, Elvis jokingly remarked at the end of his show, "I'll see you backstage." Fifty girls believed him and chased him into his dressing room right to the top of a shower stall. They ripped his shirt and pulled at his pants and

Elvis and his parents enjoyed singing together. He played the piano better than the guitar, though he never had lessons or learned to read music.

boots. Elvis laughed and said, "Don't that beat all?" He told a Jacksonville disc jockey it was "great, wonderful, fantastic, being in the center of all that noise and excitement."[9]

Elvis became almost too comfortable with his popularity. At one show in Richmond, Virginia, he burped into the mike and spit his chewing gum into the audience. He told inappropriate jokes. This time a representative from a big record company was in the audience. He ignored the antics because he recognized the magic of Elvis's voice. He told the executives at the New York office of RCA Victor about Elvis Presley.

Elvis was not content being known as a country singer. At home he listened to stacks of records by African-American singers like Ray Charles, Big Joe Turner, and Big Mama Thornton. He went to Beale Street in Memphis and soaked up the sounds of blues and jazz. His observations and study of music were evident on his next record, "Mystery Train." This song was written by Sam Phillips for African-American blues singer Little Junior Parker. Elvis used all he had learned, mixed it together, and made the piece his own. He communicated the blues by using a soft, easy voice.

Elvis knew Colonel Parker had connections within the music business, so he hired Parker as his "special adviser." Immediately, Parker took over Elvis's career. He increased Elvis's income by selling portraits at every performance for a quarter each. Next, he negotiated a salary raise for Elvis on the Louisiana Hayride from $18 to $200 per show. Since country-and-western music was not as popular in other areas of the state, Parker switched Elvis's music emphases to rhythm and blues and popular.

To promote Elvis's popular music, Colonel Parker paired him with Bill Haley and the Comets. Haley had an enormously successful rock 'n' roll record called "Rock Around the Clock." This audience wanted only Haley. Seeing Elvis's disappointment at being rejected, Haley graciously complimented him and gave him advice. Haley told Elvis to sing more rhythm songs instead of the slow ballads Elvis liked to sing on tour.

Soon Elvis became too big for Sun Records to handle. The small company could not produce enough Elvis records to keep up with the demand. Plus, Phillips needed time to record his other up-and-coming stars: Johnny Cash, Carl Perkins, and Jerry Lee Lewis. Parker pressured Phillips into selling Elvis's contract. Major record companies started bidding.

After much thought and negotiations, Sam Phillips met with RCA Victor executives at his studio on Union Street. They wanted Elvis to record music that could be used on the rhythm and blues, popular, and country radio stations. On November 21, 1955, after a year and a half of nurturing Elvis's career, Phillips sold Elvis's contract. RCA Victor paid $35,000 for the right to record Elvis Presley. This was more than any record company had ever paid to buy the contract of a popular singer.

Elvis hardly grasped his new fame. When he met with his new bosses in New York, Elvis played one of his pranks. He shook an RCA executive's hand with a joke buzzer hidden in his palm.[10]

Wild Wiggler

Elvis Presley was no longer a small-town country singer. RCA Victor had the power and money to make him a huge star. With its gigantic marketing ability, RCA could guarantee that people around the world would hear Elvis Presley music. The company furnished records to jukeboxes, radio stations, and record stores.

Elvis knew this opportunity could not have happened without Colonel Parker. He wrote a letter to show his appreciation. In it he told Parker that he loved him like a father. Gladys Presley did not feel the same about Parker.[1] She sensed he was not truthful. She was right, though neither she nor Elvis knew it.

Elvis admired Parker's intelligence and had no reason to doubt him.[2] Parker never told anyone he was an illegal immigrant from Holland. Parker's real name was Andreas Cornelis van Kuijk. He had no musical background. Prior to managing singing stars, he worked as a carnival promoter. Although he had served in the military, the honorary title of colonel was given to him by a politician friend. Openly, Parker called himself a snow man, an individual who enjoyed "snowing" people, or deceiving them. Elvis did not care. Parker had made it possible for him to quickly become a professional musician.

Colonel Parker and Elvis worked together like a pair of magicians. Opportunities seemed to appear out of nowhere and turned to gold. On Elvis's twenty-first birthday, Elvis told a reporter he could not sleep because he was so scared about how fast things were happening to him.[3]

Gladys Presley feared for her son's health and safety. If he continued to work at such a hectic pace, she warned, he would not live to be thirty.[4] She felt Parker was pushing Elvis too hard. Elvis was recording songs for RCA, performing on the Louisiana Hayride, and touring. She wanted Elvis to settle down, to buy a furniture store and get married.

Elvis could not slow down. No longer recording in Memphis, he traveled to the RCA studios in New York City and Nashville, Tennessee. At these sessions, Scotty Moore and Bill Black still accompanied him, along with three new musicians and a backup singing group. The musicians were Chet Atkins, rhythm guitarist; Floyd Cramer, pianist; and D. J. Fontana, drummer. The Jordanaires quartet sang the "oohs" and "aaahs" in the background.

Elvis liked to joke around with his manager, Colonel Tom Parker.

Elvis could not read music, but he easily memorized new songs. One of the first songs he chose to learn was "Heartbreak Hotel." It was a tale about a man losing his girlfriend and checking into a hotel filled with lonely people. To get an echo effect, he recorded the song in a stairwell. Elvis's tenor voice dipped to baritone as he sang the somber lyrics. His bluesy rock approach was intensified by the tinkle of piano keys and the heartbeat thump of the bass. Moore's and Atkins's electric guitars filled up the interludes with a soulful sound. Elvis was pleased with his record and bragged that it would sell a million copies.

Parker also had an optimistic outlook. He knew that if he could put Elvis on television, the singer's fame would spread. America's 35 million television screens offered better exposure than Elvis could get traipsing all over the country. Parker used a variety program called *Stage Show* for Elvis's first appearance. It featured 1940s music and big bands. The number of viewers watching the show had been declining. On January 28, 1956, Parker presented Elvis Presley, his "atomic-powered singer," to America. From that moment on, *Stage Show* and America were never the same.[5]

Elvis's tweed jacket and white tie bounced against his black shirt as he danced on the balls of his feet. His hands fluttered and his legs twitched. "Shake, rattle, and roll," he wailed, then switched midsong to "Flip, Flop, Fly." Bill Black added to the frenzy by pounding his bass and shouting, "Go go go!"

Television viewers had never seen anything like

Elvis. His fast music, senseless words, and twitching created mixed emotions. Some people switched to the *Perry Como Show* on another station. Como was the exact opposite of Elvis. He stood still, wore a cardigan sweater, and softly sang, "Catch a Falling Star."

Others could not get enough of Elvis. These new fans watched him the following Saturday night, too. This time he was even more animated as he hiccuped through "Baby Let's Play House." His third appearance featured the songs "Heartbreak Hotel" and "Blue Suede Shoes." In the next three weeks, his single record of "Blue Suede Shoes" sold 400,000 copies, and an album that included "Heartbreak Hotel" sold 300,000. This was the biggest-selling album in RCA history at that time.

Elvis's uninhibited music, good looks, and seductive voice intrigued the teenagers. In the 1950s, youths were stuck between their parents' memories of the Great Depression and an unknown future. Conformity, education, and morality were stressed. Elvis Presley, the rebel, blew the lid off conformity. Boys imitated his hair and dress. In Memphis, teens went to Lansky's, where Elvis bought his clothes, and begged for Elvis's clothing styles.

For the first time in history, American youths had buying power. America's World War II veterans had good jobs. They gave their children weekly allowances. Teens spent their money on the newly invented portable phonograph. Instead of listening to the juke box, they could buy the cheaper and smaller records to play at home. Elvis was the youngest and the wildest rock 'n' roll singer. Teens loved his music.

Elvis bought his jazzy clothes from Bernard Lansky, who today calls himself the "Clothier of the King." Framed on the wall behind Lansky is a pink leather coat with a mink collar that Elvis forgot to pick up after having it altered.

Parents and politicians worried that rock 'n' roll was undermining the nation's morals. They called rock 'n' roll an unleashed monster. Some Americans blamed the country's change of morals, dress, and politics on Elvis and his music. Still, Elvis mania and rock 'n' roll could not be stopped.

Other singers followed Elvis's wild style. All across America, rock 'n' roll popped up. Blacks and whites started performing together. In parts of the South, segregation laws were maintained by separating the two audiences with chicken wire. In San Antonio, Texas, public swimming pools banned the playing of rock 'n' roll music on the jukeboxes because it attracted what they considered undesirable elements. Some thought that this music gave young hoodlums an excuse to gather. One radio disc jockey publicly burned six hundred Presley records.[6]

Every month, Elvis recorded new songs. Fans bought millions. Elvis continuously defended himself and his music. He told reporters that he could not understand the uproar about his movements. He claimed they could not be bad because his mother approved. He maintained that he was a good person who went to church and did not drink or smoke.

There was no turning back. By March 1956, Elvis had made an unprecedented accomplishment. He was the best-selling artist in three musical categories, with hit records in pop, country, and rhythm and blues. The album containing "Blue Suede Shoes" became RCA's first million-selling album.

Elvis earned more money than the Presleys ever imagined. He bought a ranch-style house for his family in a nice Memphis suburb. Unlike some stars, Elvis did not hide from his fans. He had a low brick-and-wrought-iron fence built with musical notes welded onto it. He put a mailbox out front with "Presley" printed clearly. Over the front windows, he added awnings inscribed with a large letter "P."[7]

Inside, he decorated in a musical theme. He installed wallpaper covered in musical notes. Star-shaped light fixtures provided him with light as he played on one of the two pianos he had bought.[8]

He gave his mother a very special gift. It was a pink-and-white Cadillac. Back when the Presleys had little money, Gladys Presley had told Elvis about the most beautiful car she had ever seen. Her new car looked exactly like the one she had described. She cherished the gift and Elvis's thoughtfulness, but she never learned how to drive.

Gladys Presley did not let her son's fame affect her. She continued taking care of him just like any other mother. In her modern kitchen she cooked Elvis's favorite foods of meatloaf or fried banana, peanut butter, and bacon sandwiches.

She also fed the fans who waited outside for a chance to see Elvis. Daily, Elvis signed autographs. That was not enough. Fans collected dirt from his yard and stole his family's clothes right off the clothesline. One girl put a stethoscope against the outside wall of his bedroom, hoping to hear him snore.

Neighborhood kids adored Elvis, while their parents detested the constant noise and traffic. When Elvis rode his new Harley-Davidson motorcycle in the vacant lot next to his house, they ganged together to

Elvis and the great blues guitarist B. B. King in 1957: The African-American audience went wild when Elvis peeked out from behind the backstage curtain at a fundraiser where King was performing.

protest. Angry neighbors told the Presleys to move; they would buy the house. Elvis exploded. He said he would buy all their houses and *they* could move.

Elvis needed time for relaxation and fun. In order to have some privacy, he began sleeping during the day and going out late at night. From midnight until the early-morning hours he rented an amusement park. There he and friends repeatedly rode the roller coaster and the bumper cars. The Rainbow Rollerdome skating rink was also a favorite hangout. Elvis skated, and he played rough war games on skates with his friends. At dawn, he would go home and try to sleep away the fear that his fame would disappear as quickly as it had appeared.[9]

Although Parker continued to manage the Hank Snow Jamboree, he found time to create a scheme to get Elvis into the movies. He arranged for Elvis to give performances at movie theaters in Florida. These theaters were owned by Paramount Movie Studios. When Elvis played and sang between the movie showings from two in the afternoon until eleven at night, more people came to the movies. Hal Wallis, a Paramount movie producer, noticed the positive reaction to Elvis.[10] Just as Parker had planned, Wallis asked Elvis to come to Hollywood and audition to be in the movies.

On March 26, 1956, Elvis arrived in Hollywood, California. As he descended the steps from the plane, the camera around his neck bounced against his chest. A warm breeze blew his long blond hair into his face. He looked more like a tourist than a man on the verge of superstardom.

Elvis auditioned at Paramount Movie Studios by acting in a skit, then lipsynching to "Blue Suede Shoes" while holding a toy guitar. Hal Wallis was mesmerized by Elvis's electrifying performance. Colonel Parker negotiated a three-picture contract. Elvis would earn $100,000 for his first picture. The next two would increase his earnings by $50,000 each.

With this new turn of events, Elvis and Colonel Parker decided Parker should become Elvis's full-time manager. Under the conditions of the agreement, Parker would sell Elvis as he would a product. Parker's fee was 25 percent of Elvis's earnings. Elvis did not know that most managers took only 15 percent.

On April 11,1956, Elvis received his first gold record for "Heartbreak Hotel," selling one million copies just as he had predicted. The record was presented to him at the studio. Gladys Presley hung it in her wood-paneled den next to Elvis's high school diploma.

The next month, Elvis started touring as the star of his own group. Other singers did not travel with him. Jugglers and comics opened his show. Being the star, Elvis began to act crazier and crazier on stage. At a Minnesota concert, the audience was so appalled by his sexual movements that the director of the Federal Bureau of Investigation (FBI), J. Edgar Hoover, was notified. Hoover started investigating Elvis for ruining the minds and morals of American youth.

Time and *Newsweek* magazines called him the teenagers' hero. They praised his ability to sing all types of music well. In the article, Elvis humbly stated that he hoped his hometown friends did not think he had forgotten them.[11]

Elvis's next television appearance was on June 5, 1956, on a popular television variety program called the *Milton Berle Show.* Forty million people watched this show. Elvis, without a guitar, sneered, wiggled, squirmed, and knelt on the stage while singing "You Ain't Nothing But a Hound Dog." Even Scotty Moore and Bill Black were shocked by Elvis's overt sexual movements.

Life magazine called Elvis "a howling hillbilly success," although the public felt differently. Newspapers, radios, and ministers expressed their outrage at his performance. Elvis defended his style. He said, "Some people tap their feet, some people snap their fingers, and some people sway back and forth. I just sorta do 'em all together, I guess."[12] He privately explained to a friend that he could not help the way he acted. He said that when he sang, "It's like a surge of electricity that goes all through you."[13]

The more publicity Elvis got, the more the prominent television show hosts vied to book him on their variety shows. A month after the *Milton Berle Show,* Steve Allen scheduled Elvis on his show, but he promised his audience that Elvis would not give an obscene performance. To restrict Elvis, Allen required him to wear a tuxedo and blue suede shoes. To add to Elvis's humiliation, he had to stand in one spot and serenade a live hound dog with the song "You Ain't Nothing But a Hound Dog." In defiance, Elvis shook his shoulders, twitched his fingers, and snarled to rile the audience. After the show, Elvis's fans picketed the

Elvis liked his fans and cheerfully signed autographs. Some fans started an Elvis for President campaign.

television studio, carrying signs that demanded, "We want the real Presley. We want the gyratin' Elvis."

The "real Presley" loved touring and playing in front of a live audience. A North Carolina reporter witnessed one of his performances and wrote, "He slouches; he scratches; he mugs; he bumps; he grinds; the frenzy, the hysteria, the wild and wonderful shrieks of sheer joy."[14]

Elvis's performances grew more risqué and the audiences more wild. In Jacksonville, Florida, a judge ordered him to tone down his show or be arrested. To comply, Elvis wiggled only his little finger—and got the same hysterical response from the crowd.

Some skeptics believed Elvis was a fad. However, his talent and perseverance kept him on top. He always strove to be the best. For example, at one recording session, Elvis took seven hours to record two songs. He did not reach perfection until he sang "Hound Dog" thirty-one times. "Don't Be Cruel" took twenty-eight tries.

All that hard work paid off. Fans bought a million copies of each. Elvis's record career was like a runaway train. Nothing could stop it. His childhood dreams were coming true faster than he had ever expected. Now he would focus on becoming a movie star.

Hollywood Hero

In the middle of August 1956, Elvis boarded a train to Hollywood, California. He took along two cousins and three friends. On the train he memorized the entire script for his first movie, *The Reno Brothers*. Later the title was changed to *Love Me Tender*, after the ballad Elvis sings in the movie. When his fans heard about this song, they preordered 856,327 copies before it was played on the radio. Elvis earned another gold record before the song or the movie was released. Elvis found acting hard work. He called his friend in Memphis and complained that he spent all day "plowing behind a team of mules."[1]

A month later, Elvis left Hollywood to return to his hometown of Tupelo to celebrate Elvis Presley Day.

With banners and fanfare, a parade marched down Main Street. Store windows displayed hound dogs and blue suede shoes. Escorted by police, Elvis drove a white Lincoln onto the fairgrounds where he had performed when he was ten years old.

Twenty thousand people attended the concert. One hundred National Guardsmen and forty police officers tried to control the unruly crowd. A girl jumped onto the stage and hugged Elvis until guards dragged her away. Another ripped a silver button off his velvet shirt. Fans tore footlights from their sockets. In the Mississippi heat, fainting fans barely escaped being trampled.

Elvis gave his $10,000 earnings back to the city to be used to help fund the building of the Elvis Presley Youth Center behind the house where he was born. He stipulated that the money was not to be used to buy the land. Elvis did not want any of his money to go to the landowner, Orville Bean. So the city officials forced Bean to sell his land to them. The man who had pressed charges against Elvis's father and evicted Elvis and his mother from their home now lost his land to the Elvis Presley Youth Center.[2]

Elvis toured the South before going to New York to appear on the *Ed Sullivan Show*. This was a respected Sunday-night family television program. Sullivan had booked Elvis for three performances. On the first two evenings, Elvis sang, bumped and wiggled. His third performance, on January 6, 1957, was censored because of all the negative publicity he had gotten. Although the studio audience in New York could see Elvis's wiggling legs and swerving hips, the television

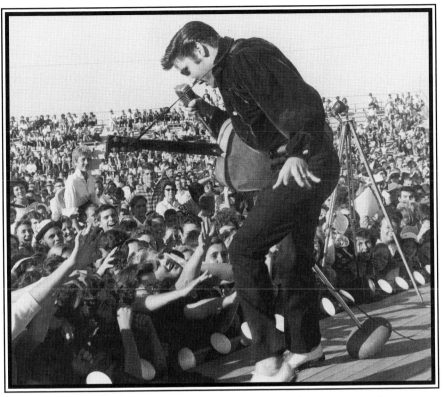

Elvis thrilled his hometown fans at the Tupelo fairgrounds.

cameras did not broadcast Elvis from the waist down. Next Elvis sang a slow religious type song titled "Peace in the Valley." Sullivan, impressed by Elvis's politeness, announced to the 54 million viewers, "This is a real decent, fine boy."[3]

Because of the song and Sullivan's kind words, more people accepted Elvis's unique style. RCA Victor released seven of Elvis's songs at one time. Elvis became the king of the airways. Every time the radio was turned on, listeners heard Elvis Presley. Because of this mass marketing, 1.6 million records were sold. The fans spent eighty-nine cents per record. Elvis earned seven cents from each sale. For five months, no other recording artist but Elvis was making the best hits charts.

Colonel Tom Parker never let the public forget Elvis. He made a deal with a merchandiser to make seventy-eight different Elvis products, including clothes, jewelry, school supplies, a game, a drink, and bubble-gum cards.

Dressing Elvis as a star was a little more difficult. After Parker paid $2,500 for a suit for Elvis, the star complained that he did not feel "cool" wearing it. He said he felt like a clown. Elvis wore the twenty-five-pound gold-lamé suit only twice.[4]

Despite Elvis's reaction to the gaudiness of the suit, he did not balk when Gladys Presley asked him to buy a huge colonial mansion. On the outskirts of Memphis, surrounded by thirteen acres of wooded land, the house sat majestically on a hill. Twenty-two-year-old Elvis purchased the run-down mansion for $102,500.[5]

The previous owners had named it Graceland after their aunt Grace. Elvis kept the name. He hired a personal decorator to modernize the house. Inside, Elvis filled the purple-and-gold living room with luxurious furniture. His bedroom was painted a very dark blue. The basement became a place where guests made milk shakes and played music on a jukebox. A turkey, hogs, chickens, peacocks, and donkeys roamed the backyard.

Elvis had to leave Graceland while he filmed his

Elvis filled Graceland with everything money could buy: a movie theater, indoor racquet ball court, entertainment room with wall-to-wall television sets, and a huge slot-car track.

second movie. In Hollywood, he stayed at the Knickerbocker Hotel. Fans constantly climbed fire escapes or devised other ways to see him. One group, the Hotel Hounds, waited for a kiss and sang "Heartbreak Hotel" backward.[6]

In *Loving You*, Elvis portrayed a country boy turned into a singing star. Bill Black and Scotty Moore, who had been excluded from *Love Me Tender*, joined Elvis as he sang soon-to-be million-sellers like "Teddy Bear" and "Loving You." For this movie, the studio makeup artist dyed Elvis's hair and eyebrows black. Elvis added black mascara and often wore his stage makeup in public.

Elvis's next movie, *Jailhouse Rock*, was made for Metro-Goldwyn-Mayer (MGM). He received $250,000 plus half of the film's profits. This made Elvis the highest-paid movie star at that time.

A *New York Herald-Tribune* writer explained Elvis's appeal. He said Elvis was "a safety valve," meaning that teenagers could scream, holler, and let go of their emotions when they saw him in movies or in concert. Teens wanted to be just like Elvis. They thought he did not have to work hard for his success.[7]

Elvis did work hard. When he needed a break, he rented a football stadium at night. Thirty friends played football with him. They grabbed refreshments from Elvis's limousine, which was stuffed with drinks and snacks.

While making movies, Elvis continued to record songs. Some were featured in his movies, others were originals for RCA. After the success of the song "Peace in the Valley" on the *Ed Sullivan Show*, Elvis recorded an album of gospel songs. This added a new dimension to his image.

On December 20, 1957, Elvis received a draft notice from the United States government. It informed Elvis that, like other men his age, he was required to join the military. Unlike most others, however, he could have been excused from his duty because he was the main financial supporter of his family.

All branches of the service tried to entice him. They offered easy positions like entertainer or recruiter. Elvis chose the United States Army. There were two reasons for this decision. First, the army would allow him to complete the filming of the movie

Being a movie star was hard work, and Elvis enjoyed being pampered by other people on the set. His cousin Gene, right, and Colonel Parker, back, join Elvis as he checks his script on the set of Love Me Tender.

King Creole. Second, Parker thought it would improve Elvis's image for him to serve as an enlisted man with no special privileges.

Elvis feared that while he was in the army, everything would disappear. He would no longer be a star. Colonel Parker promised to keep Elvis's career alive and thriving.

8

Military Man

On March 24, 1958, in the drizzling rain at the Memphis Beale Street Enlistment office, Colonel Parker distributed balloons advertising Elvis's new movie, *King Creole.* "How do you feel about the military service?" asked one reporter. Elvis answered, "It cannot be any worse than the merry-go-round [I have] been on for the past two years." Another one wondered if Elvis's fame would survive while he was in the military. "I wish I knew," replied Elvis.[1]

After the press conference, Elvis and twelve other inductees rode in an army bus to Kennedy Veterans Hospital to get their physicals. Elvis removed his gray-and-white-checkered sports jacket, striped shirt, dark pants, and pink and black socks. Photographers snapped pictures as Elvis was weighed, dressed only in his underwear. Nervous, Elvis claimed military life would be a great experience and he hoped he could live up to people's expectations.[2]

His next stop was Fort Chaffee, Arkansas. Elvis took five hours of aptitude tests. He did not score high enough to be eligible for the officer's exam. He admitted he had never been good at arithmetic.[3] His haircut caused the most commotion of the induction. Fifty reporters took photos. Elvis blew a strand of his clipped hair toward them, "Hair today, gone tomorrow," he teased.[4]

At a café on the way to Fort Hood in Killeen, Texas, fans rushed at Elvis and tore his clothes. As he hurried out, the waitresses argued over who would keep the stool he sat on.

In boot camp, Elvis found himself away from family, friends, and fans. From the day he was born, he had been treated as special. Adjusting to being a team member was going to be difficult.[5] Elvis decided to make the most of his situation. He earned a marksman and sharpshooter badge and learned karate. He also became the acting assistant leader of his squad.

While Elvis felt isolated from the public, the public hardly knew he was gone. One weekly television show aired a comic episode in which a rock 'n' roll rookie named Elvin Pelvin got brown suede combat boots.

After basic training, Elvis returned to Graceland. He swam in his swimming pool and visited with friends and even the fans standing at the gates. He took his parents to see his new movie, *King Creole*. At night, he rented the roller rink and amusement park.

Never free from work, Elvis spent ten hours recording five songs at the RCA Nashville recording studio. These songs would be released during his two years in the military. After the session, Elvis bought a new red Lincoln convertible to drive back to the base.

Elvis's parents and his grandmother, Minnie Presley, moved into a rented house next to Fort Hood. Elvis was allowed to live with them instead of on the base. An army rule allowed a soldier to live off-base if he had family nearby that depended on him for support. Having them there kept Elvis from getting homesick. He would tease his grandmother until she gave him a playful slap to stop his antics.[6] He enjoyed simple, home-cooked meals like hot dogs and sauerkraut.

Gladys Presley still found Elvis's life troublesome. Learning that her son would be shipped to Germany made her miserable. She was also ill. Her health had been getting worse. Vernon Presley took her to her physician in Memphis. Diagnosed with a liver ailment, she was admitted into the hospital.

Elvis was given an emergency leave to go to Memphis to see his sick mother. He stayed with her until she told him to go home and rest. Gladys Presley asked a friend to watch after her boy. Then she added, "cause there're just so many people that don't care about him."[7]

Elvis left the hospital thinking his mother was improving. At 3 A.M. he got a call from his father. His mother had died. Elvis rushed back to the hospital. He and his father cried over Gladys Presley's body. "She's all I lived for," sobbed Elvis.[8]

Elvis's mother was brought from the funeral home to Graceland. In the music room, friends and relatives paid their last respects to Gladys, who was wearing a blue dress and lying in a silver casket.

At Forest Hill Cemetery, twenty-two-hundred floral arrangements from people around the world decorated the hill. Overcome with grief, Elvis tried to jump into his mother's grave, but friends restrained him. He cried and promised that if he could only have her back, he would give up all his money and dig ditches.[9]

Elvis grieved alone in his room with the shades closed. When he emerged, he wandered around the mansion carrying his mother's nightgown. Some high-ranking officers gave Elvis permission to leave the military. He refused. After two weeks of mourning, he returned to the base.

A month later, on September 22, 1958, Elvis was shipped to Germany. At the military ocean terminal in Brooklyn, New York, Elvis walked up the ramp to the USS *General Randall*. He repeated this walk eight times so that photographers could snap pictures. The army band played "Tutti Frutti," "Hound Dog" and "Don't Be Cruel" in march tempo. He told reporters he hoped they would not forget him. As the ship departed, Elvis pretended to move to the music. He jokingly rotated his shoulder, snapped his fingers, and buckled his knees.

On the ship, everyone wanted Elvis's autograph. To get privacy, he slept in the sergeant's quarters. Once out to sea, the seamen held a talent show. Elvis played the piano for the crowd of thirteen hundred men. He was not allowed to sing. Colonel Tom Parker had made an arrangement with the army. Elvis would serve in the military as a soldier, not an entertainer.

The ship docked at Bremerhaven, Germany, to the cheers of fifteen hundred Elvis fans. Elvis waved like a star, but his new job was to be a combat soldier. He became a scout jeep driver. Maintaining his jeep, reading maps, making sketches, and learning enemy tactics were part of his job. His combat unit was always kept ready for battle.

In the army, Elvis learned to use this 3.5 inch rocket launcher designed to destroy tanks.

During this period called the Cold War, American forces remained on alert to stop the spread of communism. President Dwight D. Eisenhower thought the Soviet Union might invade the country of Hungary. If that happened, Elvis's unit would fight the Soviets.

The Soviets, who knew Elvis was there, waged an anti-Elvis campaign. A communist paper called him a "Cold War weapon." The Soviet government spread the belief that listening to Elvis's music would cause crime. Russian teenagers defied their government. They paid fifteen rubles—the equivalent of $12.50—for Elvis Presley records made on discarded hospital X-ray plates.[10]

On patrol, Elvis drove his jeep, armed with a machine gun, to a town near the border of Czechoslovakia. During night guard duty, he would keep the jeep running and sit on the hood wrapped in his sleeping bag to keep warm. To stay awake, Elvis took amphetamines.[11]

Elvis's father, grandmother, and friends came to live in Germany. Again, Elvis lived off base. Everyone stayed at the luxurious Ritter's Park Hotel in Bad Homburg until Elvis and his buddies were asked to leave. The other guests complained about their hallway shaving cream and water gun fights. Elvis rented a house for his family in Bad Nauheim, Germany.

Elvis was respected and liked by the other soldiers. On Christmas Eve, he gave a gift to the men in the barracks: He sang "Silent Night." The men listened in awe and admiration. As they walked out of the barracks, they each put a hand on his shoulder to show their appreciation.[12]

"The girl he left behind": Priscilla Beaulieu is about to listen to an Elvis record on the phonograph. Each side of the album held about six songs.

Elvis received ten thousand fan letters a week from around the world. Outside his home, he signed autographs every night at 7:30. After the signing, he would entertain guests at his house. One night a friend brought Priscilla Beaulieu to meet Elvis. Priscilla had recently moved with her military father and family from Texas to Germany. At her Texas school, fourteen-year-old Priscilla had been voted the most beautiful and best-dressed girl. Elvis, struck by her beauty, began inviting her to his house. Her parents approved, as long as Elvis's grandmother or father chaperoned.

On February 11, 1960, Elvis earned his full army stripes to be a sergeant. At the celebration party, Elvis proudly said, "People were expecting me to mess up, to goof up. They thought I couldn't take it and I was determined to go to any limits to prove otherwise."[13]

A month later Elvis left Germany on a military plane to return to Memphis. Newspaper photographers took Priscilla's picture as she waved good-bye. Reporters called her "the girl he left behind." Elvis denied there was anything special between him and the teenager. He knew Colonel Parker would not approve.

Parker had kept his promise. While Elvis served in the military, RCA released the recordings Elvis had made before leaving. Elvis would return to his career even more famous than before. He was the first singer ever to sell 18 million single records.

Difficult Days

Elvis Presley arrived at McGuire Air Force Base near Fort Dix, New Jersey, on March 3, 1960, in the middle of a snowstorm. After his arrival, a white limousine whisked him away to a hotel. Forty cars filled with fans, reporters, and photographers followed him. The Memphis newspapers offered a cash prize to the reporter who received the first interview with Elvis.

Elvis, Colonel Parker, and friends took a private train car to Memphis. Elvis waved from the back of the train to fans at each station. Two hundred reporters and fans braved the snow and wind to welcome Elvis back to Memphis at seven in the morning. Elvis shook hands over the wire fence.

The Memphis police chief drove him up the long

driveway to Graceland, Elvis's castle on the hill. "The king was once again on his throne," reported the *Memphis Press-Scimitar.*[1] At an afternoon press conference, a reporter asked Elvis if two years of sobering army life had changed his mind about rock 'n' roll. Elvis replied, "No, it hasn't. Because I was in tanks a long time, you see, and they rock and roll quite a bit."[2]

Elvis resumed his former pattern of sleeping all day and playing all night. In the early evening he would dine on a huge breakfast—a dozen-egg omelet, burnt bacon, and coffee. After a welcome-home party, Elvis tried to recapture the old days by going with his friends to the movie theater and amusement park, then roller skating at the rink until dawn.

Despite his efforts, he was no longer the wild teen rebel. Two years of military discipline had changed Elvis into a responsible adult. He now had two paying jobs: recording songs for RCA and starring in movies for Paramount.

America had changed too. Teens of all races listened to all types of music, from folk to popular. They freely bought records of African-American and white rock 'n' roll singers. Elvis realized his competition was stronger now than when he first started.

After a thirteen-day break, Elvis drove to the RCA Nashville recording studio B. Apprehensive about recording, he sent out for hamburgers, milk, and fries for all the musicians. After he ate, he gave a karate demonstration of the moves he had learned in the army.

Finally, he sorted through the new songs that he

was to consider recording. Elvis worked on six songs and tossed the rest aside. Being a perfectionist, he sometimes redid a song nineteen times. Elvis felt most comfortable with "Stuck On You." It had a rock 'n' roll beat similar to "All Shook Up." The next song, "Fame and Fortune," had a doo-wop rhythm. RCA Victor, excited to get new material, immediately made 1.4 million copies of a single with these two songs on it. In three weeks, "Stuck on You" hit number one and "Fame and Fortune" reached number seventeen on the charts of the top selling music.

Parker strove to erase Elvis's previous image as an immoral teen. He wanted Elvis to project a new image of a clean-cut, sensitive young man. To do this, Parker scheduled Elvis to be on the *Frank Sinatra Show.* Sinatra had been a popular singer since 1940. He did not sing rock 'n' roll and did not care for it. Sinatra agreed to put Elvis on his show because it would increase the number of viewers to his program. Sinatra paid Elvis $125,000 for his appearance. At that time, this was the highest fee ever paid a television guest.

Elvis wore a tuxedo on his first public appearance after his army years. His hair was styled and dyed black. The songs he swapped with Sinatra were smooth and polished.[3] Audiences young and old enjoyed seeing them together. It seemed as if another era in music had passed. Elvis Presley had grown up.

During Elvis's next recording session, he worked twelve hours and recorded twelve songs. He even tried a new style. In a song with a Latin beat, "It's Now or

Never," Elvis struggled and reached high operatic notes he was not used to singing.[4]

Two weeks later Elvis, Parker, and friends boarded two private railroad cars on the Southern Pacific Sunset. They were on their way back to Hollywood, California, to make movies.

While in Germany, Elvis had begun filming *G.I. Blues*. Now he was going to complete the movie. He was playing a military man stationed in Germany. The movie director enjoyed working with Elvis because Elvis listened and followed instructions.[5] During the filming, a king, a queen, and princesses from four different countries came to the movie set especially to see Elvis.

While filming, Elvis took his work seriously. On breaks he relieved stress by playing pranks. He triggered a bucket of water over a door, started pie-throwing contests, and lit firecrackers. In his hotel room at the Beverly Wilshire, he teased the bellman by removing all the furniture from the room. Shocked, the bellman got the manager. When the two returned to the room, the furniture was back. Elvis and his friends thought this prank was hilarious. The hotel management did not. So Elvis rented a house for himself and some friends.

Elvis's group of eight to nine friends followed him everywhere. Five were paid for odd jobs such as managing travel schedules or preparing Elvis's clothes. They acted as court jesters, agreeing with Elvis, laughing at his jokes, and meeting his every demand. During his first days in Hollywood, Elvis required the men to wear dark suits and sunglasses.

A bystander saw them dressed alike and asked if they were in the Mafia. She had mistaken them for a group of notorious gangsters. Since this group was from Memphis, the press started calling Elvis's friends the "Memphis Mafia."[6]

The Memphis Mafia followed Elvis to the set of his next movie, *Flaming Star*. Elvis played a boy coping with the cultural difficulties of having a Native American mother and a white father. Elvis enjoyed performing a dramatic part and sang only two songs. However, the film did not make as much money as the traditional Elvis movies. Films written especially for Elvis had a musical comedy plot, fourteen songs, girls and a romantic location. These were the movies Elvis fans wanted to see.

Blue Hawaii, Elvis's next movie, was the biggest film success in his career. Filmed in Hawaii, it showcased the newest state in America. The sound track sold well because it contained a mixture of humorous, rock, and ballad tunes. One song from this movie, "Can't Help Falling in Love," sold millions of copies, and Elvis frequently sang it at concerts.

Each success brought more deals. Colonel Parker signed Elvis for five more movies with Paramount and four pictures with MGM, which increased his salary from $200,000 to $500,000, plus 50 percent of the profits.

Between movies, Elvis and friends drove a Dodge mobile home seventeen hundred miles to Graceland. Vernon Presley had remarried and lived there with his new wife, Dee Standly. Elvis resented his father's second marriage. But he told a reporter that as long

In the posters for Elvis's movies, he was always surrounded by lots of girls.

Elvis kept a stable of horses at Graceland. He liked to ride his favorite horse, Rising Sun, down to the guarded front gates of the mansion to sign autographs for his fans.

as Dee Standly understood that he had only one mother, there would be no trouble.[7] Elvis was more cordial to Standly's three young boys, David, Billy, and Ricky. He welcomed his stepbrothers by filling the backyard with toys.[8]

With the money he had made from selling 75 million records, Elvis also amused himself with cars. He owned more than thirty vehicles. His assortment included go-carts, a black Rolls-Royce Silver Cloud, Cadillacs, Lincolns, imported sports cars, limousines, convertibles, Harley-Davidsons, and a three-wheeled Messerschmitt. In the early-morning hours, Elvis would select one and cruise around Memphis. The local police, notified by the Graceland guards, would keep watch over Elvis as he roamed the empty streets.[9]

Elvis also bought a chimpanzee named Scatter. Sometimes he dressed Scatter like a human and took him in a car. The chimp would sit on the driver's lap behind the steering wheel. When another car passed, the driver ducked down. It would look like Scatter was driving. Elvis laughed at the other driver's reaction.

Restless when he was not performing, Elvis often entertained himself by driving his go-cart around the Graceland driveway.

February 25, 1962, was declared Elvis Presley Day throughout the state of Tennessee. Elvis returned to the stage after an absence of three years to celebrate the occasion. For the first half of the show, a series of tap dancers, jugglers, acrobats, and musicians entertained. When Elvis appeared onstage, the audience applauded for three minutes. Then he performed for almost an hour.

When Elvis returned to Hollywood, he had to adjust his sleeping habits to fit the filming schedule. To get up early and work all day, he took prescription drugs. The doctors on the set of *Follow That Dream* prescribed Dexedrine diet pills (amphetamines) to wake up the actors and Valium (an antianxiety tranquilizer) to help them sleep.

In June 1962, Priscilla Beaulieu, Elvis's girlfriend from Germany, visited for two weeks. She came again in December. Elvis gave Priscilla amphetamines and sleeping pills to help her adjust to his schedule. She went skating, saw movies, and rode the roller coaster till dawn. Elvis lavished her with clothes and paid for her to get a total makeover. He convinced her to dye her brown hair black. She styled it in a 1960s beehive hairdo. Twenty-six-year-old Elvis made Priscilla appear much older than her sixteen years.

Priscilla returned to Germany, and Elvis kept making films. He was dissatisfied and embarrassed by the poor quality of the movie songs. Sometimes he had to sing ridiculous songs to a puppet or bull. The RCA recording selections were not much better. For the first time in seven years, Elvis did not have a hit.

He became interested in medicines and began

reading the *Physicians' Desk Reference*, a medical reference book. He used his knowledge to acquire more prescription pills. While Elvis experimented with these drugs, Parker kept Elvis working. "You got a product, sell it," became Colonel Parker's slogan.[10]

By the end of 1963, Elvis was the highest-paid star in Hollywood. Still, having money, fans, a girlfriend, cars, and a mansion did not make Elvis content with his life. He felt he had not achieved his true life purpose. He began reading books on religion for guidance. While reading a book on meditations, Elvis gained an insight into his life. He scribbled on the bottom of a page, "God loves you, but he loves you best when you sing."[11]

Singing had always been Elvis's passion, but movie obligations kept him from focusing on his music. Parker negotiated a fee of $1 million for one picture with MGM and five more movies with another studio. He told a *New York Times* reporter, "We're doing all right the way we are going. Every year more money rolls in."[12]

The year 1964 brought a serious challenge to Elvis's kingdom. The Beatles, a rock group from England, invaded the American music scene. Teens went wild for the Beatles just as they had for Elvis eight years earlier. Parents again reacted with disgust. The four musicians wore long bowl-cut hairstyles. They produced a new simple-lyric sound, and girls swooned at their presence. Radio stations and magazines started polling teens, asking if they preferred Elvis or the Beatles.

As if to remind the Beatles of his royal status, Elvis

sent them a note welcoming them to America and wishing them luck. He even had them as guests at his Hollywood home. Elvis did not talk much during the visit. He fiddled with a bass connected to an amp and played along with a hit record by Charlie Rich called "Mohair Sam." Eventually he jammed a little with two of the Beatles, Paul McCartney and John Lennon. Regardless of his behavior, the Beatles felt honored— especially John Lennon, who swore Elvis was his inspiration for becoming a musician.

The Beatles did not instantly knock Elvis off his throne. In May, Elvis's movie *Viva Las Vegas* did better at the theaters than the Beatles' movie *A Hard Day's Night*. Later, Elvis's music stayed in close competition with the Beatles'. His *Roustabout* sound track album made number one on the charts the week before *The Beatles '65* album.

Besides the Beatles, other outside influences began eroding Elvis's career. America's politics and values were changing. President John F. Kennedy had been killed. The Vietnam War continued. Teens listened to protest songs and the sound track from a play called *Hair*. The play's vulgar language and sexual subject matter made Elvis's music and moves look mild. Drugs began to infiltrate parts of American culture. In the turbulent 1960s, Elvis's movies seemed unrealistic and silly. His fame began to slip.

After nineteen movies, thirty-year-old Elvis Presley began to reevaluate his future. He started experimenting with LSD and cocaine. He became moody and edgy, and he lost his temper easily.

When Beatlemania hit America, Elvis had a tough time accepting second place on the movie marquee.

Colonel Parker complained, "I'm having trouble with the boy. He's changing."[13]

Parker did not change. He did his job. Since Elvis could learn scripts so quickly, the movie studios sped up production. One film, *Harum Scarum,* was made in only fifteen days. As the quality of the movies decreased, so did the number of viewers. Elvis the perfectionist resented being rushed through these movies.

While filming his twentieth movie, *Paradise Hawaiian Style,* Elvis started acting more erratically. He shot his television screens with his gun. He had his friends fill the swimming pool with flashbulbs, then he shot the bulbs. The glass-filled water had to be drained the next day. In Hawaii, he threw $5,000 in $10 and $20 bills out the window from his penthouse hotel room. He joked as couples dressed in tuxedos and evening gowns dived into the fountain after the money.[14]

Despite all this upheaval, Elvis still clung to his music. He would send friends out to purchase hit records from a Music City record store in Hollywood. Musicians visited his home for informal jam sessions.

Elvis began to mix his music with his spiritual search. He explained his feelings to a movie columnist. He said that while recording, "I feel God and his goodness, and I believe I can express his love for us in music."[15] He built a Meditation Garden near the swimming pool at Graceland. In it were stained-glass panels, statues made of Italian marble, and a fountain with fourteen different sprays and underwater lights.

It is not surprising that Elvis's next album was a

religious one. Elvis told the RCA producer in Nashville that he wanted a big sound for this album, so more backup singers and musicians were added. Singer Jake Hess watched Elvis record *How Great Thou Art.* He observed, "Elvis was one of those individuals when he sang a song he just seemed to live every word of it. He had that certain something that everyone searches for all during their lifetime."[16] This album won Elvis a Grammy Award for Best Sacred Performance.

Away from Hollywood, Elvis returned to his old self. He did not dye his hair, and he resumed a normal day-and-night cycle. He bought a ranch near Walls, Mississippi, and twenty-three horses. For his friends he bought twenty-four trucks, and house trailers for them to live in. He enjoyed the carefree lifestyle at the ranch. Not wanting to return to Hollywood, he persuaded Dr. George Nichopoulos to write him a medical excuse so he could extend his stay. The doctor wrote that Elvis had saddle sores and needed more time off to recuperate.

During this time, Priscilla and Elvis became engaged. On May 1, 1967, thirty-two-year-old Elvis Presley and twenty-one-year-old Priscilla Beaulieu shared an eight-minute ceremony at the Aladdin Hotel in Las Vegas. One hundred people attended the reception. Guests enjoyed watching the couple cut into a five-foot-high, six-tiered wedding cake decorated with pink and white roses.

Nine months later, on February 1, 1968, Lisa Marie Presley was born. Elvis proudly held his baby and admired her dark silky black hair. He said, "She's so perfect. Even the color of her hair is right," he said.[17]

Elvis and Priscilla Presley were delighted with their newborn daughter, Lisa Marie.

One hundred fans, plus patients and nurses, watched the three leave the hospital followed by caravan of Cadillacs and Lincolns.

At the end of February, the Presleys moved from Graceland to their new hilltop home in Los Angeles. Elvis's grandmother and aunt remained at Graceland. For the young family, the small, four-bedroom house in the ritzy Trousdale Estates provided the privacy they wanted while Elvis finished his film obligations and waited for new career opportunities.

Elvis's 1968 television special was "a new triumph" for the king of rock 'n' roll, according to his wife, Priscilla, and his fans.

Comeback King

Elvis starred in his own television special in June 1968. Dressed in a black leather suit, Elvis wowed the audience with his sense of humor, humility, and talent. His fans and critics called this event Elvis's 1968 comeback special. "We all knew he had a new triumph," said Priscilla. "He hadn't lost his touch, he was still the King of Rock 'n' Roll."[1] The viewing public agreed. More people watched this special than any other show of the year. Elvis's final song, "If I Can Dream," became his first million-selling record in nine years.

The success of this program inspired Elvis to get back to music. He began recording at the American Recording Studio in Memphis. The owner, Chips Moman, had worked with Neil Diamond and other new music stars. Moman helped Elvis achieve a modern sound. He added musicians playing cellos, violas, and French horns to Elvis's strong voice. In all-night sessions, Elvis recorded "In the Ghetto," "Suspicious Minds," "Kentucky Rain," and "Don't Cry Daddy." At the end of the week, he felt confident that he had regained his kingdom. To confirm his feelings, he asked Moman, "We have some hits, don't we?" "Maybe some of your biggest," Moman agreed.[2]

Pleased with Elvis's renewed enthusiasm, Colonel Parker arranged a performance at the newest and biggest hotel in Las Vegas. The International Hotel boasted the grandest showroom in the world. It seated two thousand. Only big stars could sell enough tickets to fill this room.

Elvis accepted the challenge. "I was human again," he said. "There was hope for the future. I was able to give some feeling, put some expression into my work."[3] Elvis personally prepared a musical extravaganza for the show by assembling a variety of musicians. Together, they rehearsed blues, country, gospel, and pop for the event. Meanwhile, Colonel Parker plastered Las Vegas with advertisements and filled hotels beyond capacity. Despite his team's preparation, Elvis feared the showroom would not be filled. To guarantee success, he flew in two airplanes full of friends.

On July 31,1969, two thousand celebrities and fans from all over the world jammed into the showroom. Anxiously they waited for the King to appear. Elvis paced back and forth behind the curtain, sweating in a nervous frenzy. When he heard the first notes of "Blue Suede Shoes," he stepped out onstage. Instantly, he connected with the audience. They loved him, and he loved them. He seemed to transform into the young Elvis as he sang "All Shook Up" and "Jailhouse Rock." One spectator said, "Elvis was a light coming on that stage. The electricity from the audience and the electricity from him. It was unbelievable."[4]

"Before the evening's out," said Elvis. "I'm sure I will have made a complete and utter fool of myself, but I hope you get a kick out of watching."[5]

They did. Elvis entertained for two hours, and women screamed, swooned, and begged for kisses. Men sat mesmerized by his passion, energy, and talent. The appreciative crowd honored Elvis with repeated standing ovations. It was like his concerts in the fifties.

Elvis broke a Las Vegas record when a total of 101,500 people attended his shows. No other entertainer in that city's history had ever drawn such a large audience. Colonel Parker negotiated with the hotel management for Elvis's return. They agreed to pay Elvis $1 million a year for eight weeks of work. This contract would continue until 1974.

Men and women wearing the newest fashions of miniskirts and polyester leisure suits flocked to Elvis's Las Vegas shows. His performances were spectacular. He sang current hits and wore a white jumpsuit. Long black sideburns framed his thin face.

To add to Elvis's usual stage jitters, his Saturday night show on August 29, 1970, was marred by a kidnapping threat. Elvis took it seriously. During his performance, he and his "Memphis Mafia" carried guns. An ambulance and doctor stood ready. Elvis began to keep a distance from his fans.

At the end of 1970, Elvis once again broke an attendance record. The hotel management rewarded him with a golden belt worth $10,000. Its gold, diamonds, and rubies sparkled under the spotlights. Elvis regularly wore the belt because it resembled the championship belts given to boxers and wrestlers.

Elvis's Las Vegas performances demanded a lot of him physically. Afternoon matinees and evening performances lasting until 3 A.M. were exhausting. Elvis obtained prescription drugs, including vitamin injections that contained amphetamines, from different Las Vegas doctors.

Elvis began acting in bizarre ways. He went on a three-night buying spree at Kerr's Sporting Goods, spending $20,000 on guns. He purchased cars, houses, and extravagant jewelry for friends.

One thing Elvis's money could not buy was a federal Drug Enforcement Administration badge. For years he had been collecting law enforcement badges in different cities. Some of the honorary badges actually allowed him to make an arrest. When Elvis decided he wanted a Federal Drug Enforcement Administration badge, he found it extremely difficult to obtain. After all his efforts failed, he decided to go to the president of the United States, Richard Nixon, and volunteer to be a drug enforcement agent. Elvis did not consider his own drug usage to be a problem because the drugs he took were legally prescribed by doctors.

President Nixon met Elvis in the Oval Office of the

Elvis was thrilled with the special Drug Enforcement Administration badge he received from President Richard M. Nixon.

White House. They exchanged gifts. Elvis gave Nixon an antique gun and autographed pictures. Nixon gave Elvis cuff links and other items marked with the presidential seal. Elvis explained to President Nixon how his fame and music could be of assistance to the Federal Drug Agency. President Nixon, although a little puzzled by Elvis's visit, gave him the badge. Elvis was so excited and pleased that he hugged the president.

Elvis became obsessed with his new role as a law enforcement appointee. For his birthday, he had a police radio installed in his Mercedes Benz and bought a revolving blue light. He would often stop speeding motorists. Instead of issuing tickets, he gave an autograph and lecture.[6]

Fifteen years prior, Elvis had been blamed for all of America's problems. Now a reporter asked him if today's music had a negative effect on young people. He responded, "Yes, I don't go along with music advocating drugs and desecration of the flag. I think an entertainer is for entertaining and to make people happy."[7]

Elvis had earned fifty-six gold singles and fourteen gold albums, beating the record sales of the Beatles and the Rolling Stones. He strove year after year to entertain his audiences. In his teens he had decided his fans deserved a great show. Otherwise they might as well stay home and listen to his records. Promoting this belief, Elvis made every show a spectacle of drama and flair. He would royally enter the stage to "Also Sprach Zarathustra"—music from the movie *2001: A Space Odyssey.* His costumes were dazzling jumpsuits adorned with jewels. After the show, Parker's friend Al Dvorin would announce, "Elvis has left the building."[8]

Elvis's touring performances were just as extravagant. He gave the fans what they wanted at the expense of his health. Continuous fifteen-day tours exhausted him. The strain of flying from city to city, rehearsing, dressing, performing, and flying to the next place led Elvis to take more drugs. Sleeping pills and amphetamines kept Elvis working as his earnings topped $1 million for two to three weeks of performances.

At first, Elvis seemed to be able to keep up the hectic pace. He became the first entertainer to sell out four consecutive shows at Madison Square Garden in New York City. Bob Dylan, John Lennon, and David Bowie were among the eighty thousand fans there.[9]

His family life suffered. Elvis seldom saw his family. Priscilla sent him what she called "care packages," with pictures of Lisa Marie and tape recordings of her saying new words.[10] But Elvis's absences, womanizing, and erratic celebrity behavior strained the marriage.

At the end of 1972, Priscilla informed Elvis that she wanted a divorce. She and Lisa Marie moved to California. "Man it hurts," Elvis told a friend.[11] Then he complained, "I'm tired of being Elvis Presley." He sank into depression and took more prescription medication.

To lift Elvis's spirits, Parker arranged another challenge for Elvis. He would give a major concert for fans around the world. Elvis would perform on the first television special broadcast worldwide by satellite.

On January 14, 1973, at 12:30 A.M. Elvis entertained a live audience at the Honolulu International Center. His $2,000, white-caped jumpsuit, decorated with a jeweled eagle, sparkled in the spotlights. Via satellite, Elvis dazzled more than a billion people in forty countries. The Honolulu audience adorned him with flower leis and kisses. The album of the sound track of this concert sold more than a million copies, earning Elvis his first gold album in nine years.

More than a billion people around the world watched Elvis's Aloha from Hawaii *concert on television in 1973.*

Perplexing Performer

After this colossal event in Hawaii, Elvis gave mediocre Las Vegas performances. High on drugs, he gave rambling speeches instead of singing onstage. Even as he was having difficulty standing, he swore that rumors of his taking drugs were untrue. His summer show received negative reviews. "It was one of the most disheartening performances of his Las Vegas career," said one reporter.[1]

Two months later, Elvis's doctor admitted him to the hospital in a semicomatose condition. Doctors determined that he was addicted to one of the prescription drugs he was taking. This drug abuse had damaged his liver, intestines, colon, stomach, and eyes. During his two-week stay in the hospital,

President Richard Nixon and Georgia governor Jimmy Carter called to wish him well.

Friends offered Elvis help after he was released from the hospital, but he continued to deny that he had a problem. His behavior became more and more bizarre. His moods fluctuated. One day he mistreated some longtime friends. The next day, he presented them with gifts of houses, cars, and jewelry.

Elvis desperately searched for something unique and creative to accomplish. He worked on a karate documentary for a while but never completed it. Then came the opportunity he had been waiting for throughout his career: a dramatic movie role. Barbra Streisand, the actress and producer, asked Elvis to star in her movie. It would be the remake of the 1940s movie *A Star Is Born*. Ecstatic, Elvis shared the news with everyone close to him.

Colonel Parker refused the deal because he believed that Elvis would not make enough money. Disappointed, Elvis took more drugs, further deteriorating his mind, body, and spirit. He fell face-first out of his limousine in front of fans. He had gained seventy pounds, and audiences failed to respond to his bad performances. In anger, he tossed his $2,000 rings at them.

"Elvis, Paunchy, Depressed and Living in Fear" was the new theme of articles written about him.[2] Television comedians joked about him. But Elvis kept performing. On New Year's Eve, 1975, he sang for an hour at the Silverdome in Pontiac, Michigan, and earned $300,000.[3]

At Graceland he stayed in his darkened room and

watched television for weeks at a time. He would fall asleep while eating. A fulltime nurse watched over him because twice he almost died from choking.

Physically ill with intestinal, bowel, and liver problems, Elvis continued making millions of dollars for his concerts. He spent some of it on a four-engine 880 Convair jet. Then he laid out another million dollars to have the plane's interior changed into a flying home with 14-karat-gold-plated bathroom fixtures, a bedroom, and conference room. Elvis used the plane and a five-person crew to fly anywhere he wanted to go on the spur of the moment.[4] Once he flew to Denver, Colorado, for a sandwich. With the cost of fuel and the salary of the crew, the outing cost $30,000.

RCA Victor still demanded Elvis records. When Elvis refused to go to the studio, RCA's record producer sent a truck full of electronic equipment to Graceland. Engineers set up the equipment in a den with a stone waterfall and furniture covered in fake fur. Musicians waited hours, then days, for Elvis to come downstairs from his bedroom. When he did record, he sang only sad songs. After a week, Elvis completed ten songs for an album. In April 1976 this album reached number one on the country-and-western music best-selling list.

Concert tours occupied much of Elvis's time between Las Vegas appearances. He traveled to as many as fourteen different cities in fourteen days to perform. Two- or three-day breaks were often spent at his Palm Springs, California, house, where he would race his black dune buggy, play basketball, and watch movies. Then he would take more prescription drugs to give him energy to start traveling again.

At first, Elvis's loyal fans ignored the poor quality of his concert performances. One reviewer said, "They were screaming for what he was, what he symbolizes, rather than what he is."[5] Later, fans were not as forgiving; they demanded refunds. Elvis knew he needed help. Backstage he asked a minister to pray for him. In June 1976, one fan cried for Elvis when she saw his show. She said, "He was fat, couldn't walk. . . . I really thought he was going to die."[6]

This fan was not the only one to describe Elvis honestly. Three longtime Elvis friends and members of the "Memphis Mafia"—Red West, Sonny West and Dave Hebler—wrote and published a book titled, *Elvis: What Happened?* They described bizarre behavior like his fascination with death and how he visited morgues to view corpses. They gave details about his drug abuse. Elvis was fearful of his fans' reactions, telling his cousin Billy Smith that he worried about the fans' booing or throwing things. He threatened to run away and change his identity. Another cousin reminded Elvis that if he did, he would no longer be "Elvis, the King of Rock 'n' Roll."

Not ready to relinquish his kingdom, Elvis continued to perform in Las Vegas and on long concert tours. Parker persuaded CBS to make a documentary of Elvis on tour. At the June 19, 1977, concert in Omaha, Nebraska, overweight Elvis played the piano and struggled to complete a song. He breathed heavily and sweated. The audience clapped with relief when he actually made it to the end of the song.

On August 15, 1977, Elvis went to the dentist, who gave him medication to stop the pain caused by two fillings. At home, Elvis phoned his personal physician for more medication. The doctor gave it to him.

After a short game of racquetball with friends, Elvis played his piano. He sang a few gospel songs and "Blue Eyes Crying in the Rain." At six-thirty in the morning, Elvis took his nightly dose of prescription sleeping pills then went to bed. According to Ginger Allen, his girlfriend, he woke up about 10:30 A.M. He apparently decided to read in the bathroom.

Three hours later, she found Elvis facedown on the floor with a book beside him. He was not breathing. An ambulance rushed Elvis to the hospital. His doctor and others tried to resuscitate him. Although Elvis Presley had died at Graceland a few hours before, the doctors recorded his death as 3:30 P.M. on August 16, 1977. Vernon Presley cried, "What am I going to do? Everything is gone."[7]

Maurice Elliott, a hospital administrator, made the announcement of Elvis Presley's death to reporters. Doctors stated the cause of death to be "cardiac arrhythmia due to undetermined heartbeat."[8]

Tests revealed that fourteen prescription drugs were in Elvis's system. Because of this, there was a debate among physicians about whether his death was drug-induced.

Bernard Lansky, who had sold Elvis his first snazzy clothes, dressed Elvis for the funeral in a white suit, blue shirt, and white tie.[9] A friend covered Elvis's graying hair with black dye. Elvis was ready for his last public appearance.

Every day, fans adorn Elvis's grave at Graceland with notes, flowers, and stuffed animals.

Fifty thousand fans slowly filed by the copper casket placed in Graceland's entry way. They cried and whispered loving words. One distant cousin secretly snapped a photo of Elvis in the coffin and sold it to the *National Enquirer*.

The next day, Elvis's friends and relatives shared stories. They sang Elvis's favorite hymns, "How Great Thou Art" and "My Heavenly Father Watches Over Me." The Reverend C. W. Bradley said Elvis was an example of "one human being who has strong desire and unfailing determination."[10]

Nine friends, relatives, and Memphis Mafia members carried the coffin to the hearse. The white hearse, followed by seventeen white limousines, rolled down the long driveway. A silver Cadillac led forty-nine additional cars in the procession, which was escorted by motorcycle police. Thousands of people lined Elvis Presley Boulevard.

At Forest Hill cemetery, floral arrangements in the shape of guitars, hound dogs, crowns, and broken hearts covered a hill. Elvis's body was placed in a crypt close to his mother's grave.

Eleven days later, three men attempted to steal Elvis's body from the crypt made of two layers of cement and marble. As a result, Vernon Presley had Elvis's and Gladys Presley's bodies moved to Graceland. The Meditation Garden is now their burial place. Above Elvis's gravestone sits a clear glass lamp holding an eternal flame. It flickers like the kerosene lamp that lit Elvis's birth in Tupelo, Mississippi.

The mural ALL in the Family II at East Tennessee State University shows many of the musicians—both black and white—who are linked to the history of bluegrass and country music. Elvis stands at the bottom left.

Elvis Presley's Legacy

After Elvis's death, Vernon Presley signed a contract that authorized Elvis's agent, Colonel Tom Parker, to manage Elvis's image and keep it alive.[1] Parker soon made a deal with Factor, Inc., a large merchandising company, to produce Elvis souvenirs. Millions of grieving fans were ready to spend their money on Elvis remembrances. Parker advised RCA to keep its factories open to produce millions of records to meet the new demand.

Two years later, Vernon Presley died. Elvis's ex-wife, Priscilla, along with Elvis's accountant and the Memphis National Bank of Commerce, were legally placed in charge of the Elvis empire. In 1982 they opened Graceland to the public. Listed on the National Register of Historic Places, it attracts as many people as the White House. Elvis fans eagerly pay to get a behind-the-scenes look at the royal life of the King.

On her thirtieth birthday, Lisa Marie, Elvis's daughter, inherited Graceland and Elvis's wealth. Her advisers formed a company called Elvis Presley Enterprises. It receives a percentage of the profits from the sale of any product carrying the Elvis Presley image.

The memory of Elvis, like his music, connects people all around the world. He has become an icon. His voice, image, and silhouette are internationally known. Even his name and familiar phrases serve as a secret code among Elvis fans.

United States president William Clinton's secret CIA name while in office was *Elvis*. "Thank you, thank you very much," said with Elvis's southern accent and cadence, has been mimicked since he first uttered the words onstage.

"Takin' Care of Business" is how Elvis used to describe his work. There are so many daily references to Elvis that a father and son in Mississippi take turns watching six televisions twenty-four hours a day, 365 days a year, ready to videotape references to Elvis. They also have close to twenty thousand newspaper clippings mentioning the King.[2]

Fans not only discuss Elvis, they collect anything he ever owned or touched. Collectors spend thousands of dollars on locks of his hair, his jewelry, clothes, vehicles, furniture, houses, and documents.

Tabloids with headlines stating ELVIS IS ALIVE are snatched up by hopeful people.[3] They want to believe Elvis faked his death so that he could live a private,

This bronze statue of Elvis Presley stands today on Beale Street in Memphis, where young Elvis used to go to listen to the sounds of jazz, blues, and gospel.

normal life. Dr. Jerry T. Francisco, Memphis coroner, knows this is not true. He says Elvis's brain and heart are still in storage at Memphis Baptist Memorial Hospital.[4]

Inspired by Elvis's determination and success, many view Elvis as an example of the American dream fulfilled. Elvis began his life in poverty and ended it with billions of dollars.[5] To be like him, fans have become Elvis impersonators. Thirty-five thousand Elvis impersonators have appeared since 1977.

Governments worldwide have also kept the Elvis legend alive. More than forty-six countries issued postage stamps with Elvis's image. Grenada started the trend in 1978. Fifteen years later, Elvis became the first rock star to be honored by a United States postage stamp. It is the best-selling U.S. stamp, having sold more than 517 million copies. Elvis currency has also been produced. In 1992 the Republic of the Marshall Islands became the first government to issue Elvis Presley coins as a legal money form.

Elvis Presley once confided to a friend that he feared no one would remember him. He need not have worried. Colonel Parker sold Elvis as if he were a product, and this marketing continues today. Elvis's image appears on phone cards, cartoons, and commercials. In the year 2003, his empire made $40 million—making him, according to *Forbes* magazine, the wealthiest deceased celebrity in the world for the third year in a row.

Elvis never seemed to grasp the effect he had on music and the American culture. Elvis Presley, the rebel, almost put country music out of business.

He rocketed rock 'n' roll around the world. His rebellious image nourished the seed of individuality within conforming teens and unleashed pent-up feelings in others.

The 2 billion records Elvis sold during his life, if put end to end, would circle the earth twice.[6] He starred in thirty-three movies and performed thousands of concerts. The United States National Archives featured Elvis Presley in its exhibit "American Originals."

"They really liked me, Miss Scrivener. They really liked me," Elvis said after his high school talent show.[7] He could never have predicted how much audiences would always like and treasure him. Elvis Presley dreamed of being a singer and a movie star. He never imagined he would reign forever as the King of Rock 'n' Roll.

Chronology

1935—Born in Tupelo, Mississippi, on January 8.

1946—Receives his first guitar.

1948—Presley family moves to Memphis, Tennessee.

1953—Graduates from Humes High School.

1954—Records "That's All Right (Mama)" and "Blue Moon of Kentucky"; signs recording contract with Sun Records.

1955—Colonel Tom Parker becomes Elvis's manager; Elvis signs with RCA Victor.

1956—"Heartbreak Hotel" single and Elvis Presley album are released; Elvis signs seven-year movie contract with Paramount Movie Studios; appears on TV on the Ed Sullivan Show.

1957—Purchases Graceland mansion.

1958—Inducted into the U.S. Army; mother, Gladys Presley, dies on August 14.

1959—Meets Priscilla Beaulieu.

1960—Discharged from military service.

1967—Wins his first Grammy Award, for "How Great Thou Art"; marries Priscilla.

1968—Daughter, Lisa Marie, is born on February 1; Elvis ('68 Comeback Special) airs on television.

1969—Begins performing at the International Hotel in Las Vegas, Nevada; touring for the first time since 1957.

1970—Meets with President Richard M. Nixon at the White House.

1971—Birthplace in Tupelo, Mississippi, opens to the public; Elvis continues to tour.

1972—Four New York concert dates sell out Madison Square Garden.

1973—*Elvis: Aloha from Hawaii* televised concert is seen by over 1.5 billion people; Elvis and Priscilla are divorced.

1976—Makes final Las Vegas appearance at the Hilton.

1977—Gives last concert in Indianapolis, Indiana; dies at Graceland on August 16.

Discography and Filmography

A Selected List

HIT SINGLES

Heartbreak Hotel, 1956

Blue Suede Shoes, 1956

Don't Be Cruel, 1956

Hound Dog, 1956

Love Me Tender, 1956

All Shook Up, 1957

(Let Me Be Your) Teddy Bear, 1957

Loving You, 1957

Jailhouse Rock, 1957

I Beg of You, 1957

Wear My Ring Around Your Neck, 1958

Hard-Headed Woman, 1958

One Night, 1958

(Now and Then There's) A Fool Such As I, 1959

I Need Your Love Tonight, 1959

A Big Hunk O' Love, 1959

Are You Lonesome Tonight?, 1960

Little Sister, 1961

Good Luck Charm, 1962

Return to Sender, 1962

(You're the) Devil in Disguise, 1963

Puppet on a String, 1965

The Wonder of You/Mama Liked the Roses, 1970

Burning Love, 1972

Pop Albums

Elvis Presley, 1956

Elvis, 1956

Jailhouse Rock, 1957

King Creole, 1958

Elvis Is Back!, 1960

His Hand in Mine, 1961

Something for Everybody, 1961

Girl Happy, 1965

How Great Thou Art, 1967

From Elvis in Memphis, 1969

From Memphis to Vegas, From Vegas to Memphis (2-disc set), 1969

Elvis Country, 1971

Elvis at Madison Square Garden, 1972

Elvis—Aloha from Hawaii, 1973

Elvis in Concert, 1977

Moody Blue, 1977

FILMOGRAPHY

Love Me Tender, 1956

Jailhouse Rock, 1957

G.I. Blues, 1960

Blue Hawaii, 1961

Follow That Dream, 1961

Girls! Girls! Girls!, 1962

It Happened at the World's Fair, 1963

Fun in Acapulco, 1963

Kissin' Cousins, 1964

Viva Las Vegas, 1964

Roustabout, 1964

Girl Happy, 1964

Tickle Me, 1965

Harum Scarum, 1965

Paradise, Hawaiian Style, 1966

Frankie and Johnny, 1966

Spinout, 1966

Easy Come, Easy Go, 1967

Double Trouble, 1967

Clambake, 1967

Stay Away, Joe, 1968

Speedway, 1968

Live a Little, Love a Little, 1968

Charro!, 1969

Change of Habit, 1969

The Trouble With Girls, 1969

Chapter Notes

Chapter One. Presley Power

1. Peter Guralnick, *Last Train to Memphis* (Boston: Little, Brown, 1984), p, 51.

2. Jerry Hopkins, *Elvis* (New York: Simon and Schuster, 1971), p. 377.

3. Peter Guralnick and Ernst Jorgensen, *Elvis Day by Day* (New York: Ballantine Books, 1999), p. 11.

4. Guralnick, *Last Train to Memphis*, p. 53.

5. Hopkins, p. 42.

6. Ibid.

7. Guralnick and Jorgensen, p. 12.

Chapter Two. Tupelo Talent

1. Peter Guralnick, *Last Train to Memphis* (Boston: Little, Brown, 1994), p. 13.

2. Ibid., p. 29.

3. Elaine Dundy, *Elvis and Gladys* (New York: Dell Publishing, 1985), p. 80.

4. Ibid., p. 92.

5. Ibid., p. 108.

6. Chris Davidson, "50 Facts about Elvis," *Elvis An American Legend* (Beverly Hills: L.F.P. Inc, 1995), p. 53.

7. Dundy, p. 105.

8. Guralnick, *Last Train to Memphis*, p. 28.

9. Peter Guralnick and Ernst Jorgensen, *Elvis Day by Day* (New York Ballantine Books, 1999), p. 7.

10. Dundy, p. 145.

Chapter Three. Memphis Music

1. Peter Guralnick, *Last Train to Memphis* (Boston: Little Brown and Company, 1994), p. 36.

2. Ibid.

3. Cindy Hazen and Mike Freeman, *Memphis Elvis-Style* (Winston-Salem, North Carolina: John F. Blair, 1997), p. 26.

4. Guralnick, p. 41.

5. Peter Guralnick and Ernst Jorgensen, *Elvis Day by Day* (New York: Ballantine Books, 1999), p. 8.

6. Elaine Dundy, *Elvis and Gladys* (New York: Dell Publishing, 1985), p. 158.

7. Guralnick, p. 41.

8. Ibid., p. 324.

9. Ibid., p. 51.

10. Rose Clayton and Dick Heard, *Elvis Up Close* (Atlanta, Georgia: Turner Publishing, 1994), p. 35.

11. Clayton and Heard, p. 38.

12. Guralnick and Jorgensen, p. 12.

Chapter Four. Sun Sound

1. Sun Studio Tour – August 23, 2001.

2. Peter Guralnick, *Last Train to Memphis* (Boston: Little Brown and Company, 1994), p 63.

3. Jerry Hopkins, *Elvis* (New York: Simon and Schuster, 1971), p. 66.

4. Guralnick, p. 63.

5. Ibid., p. 68.

6. Ibid., p. 84.

7. Ibid., p. 85.

8. Hopkins, p. 74.

9. Elaine Dundy, *Elvis and Gladys* (New York: Dell Publishing, 1985), p. 244.

Chapter Five. Rockabilly Rebel

1. Peter Guralnick, *Last Train to Memphis* (Boston: Little, Brown, 1994), p. 104.

2. Elaine Dundy, *Elvis and Gladys* (New York: Dell Publishing, 1985), p. 197.

3. Guralnick, p. 105.

4. Peter Guralnick and Ernst Jorgensen, *Elvis Day by Day* (New York: Ballantine Books, 1990), p. 21.

5. Guralnick, p. 131.

6. Jerry Hopkins, *Elvis* (New York: Simon and Schuster, 1971), p. 78.

7. Guralnick, p. 143.

8. Rose Clayton and Dick Heard, *Elvis Up Close* (Atlanta, Georgia: Turner Publishing, 1994), p. 90.

9. Clayton and Heard, p. 74.

10. Guralnick, p. 242.

Chapter Six. Wild Wiggler

1. Elaine Dundy, *Elvis and Gladys* (New York: Dell Publishing, 1985), p. 283.

2. Jerry Hopkins, *Elvis* (New York: Simon and Schuster, 1971), p. 156.

3. Peter Guralnick, *Last Train to Memphis* (Boston: Little, Brown, 1994), p. 249.

4. Dundy, p. 283.

5. Alanna Nash, *Elvis Aaron Presley: Revelations from the Memphis Mafia* (New York: Harper Collins, 1995), p. 67.

6. Hopkins, p. 143.

7. Author interview with Mike Freeman, author and Elvis biographer who lives in Elvis's Audubon Drive house, August 2001.

8. Mike Freeman interview.

9. Peter Guralnick and Ernst Jorgensen, *Elvis Day By Day* (New York: Ballantine Books, 1999), p. 102.

10. Hopkins, 129.

11. Guralnick, p. 277.

12. *Pages of Time* pamphlet (Millersville, Tenn.: Elvis Presley Enterprises, Inc., 2000), p. 5.

13. June Juanico, *Elvis—In the Twilight of Memory* (New York, Arcade Publishing, 1997), p. 196.

14. Guralnick and Jorgensen, p. 62.

Chapter Seven. Hollywood Hero

1. Peter Guralnick and Ernst Jorgensen, *Elvis Day by Day* (New York: Ballantine Books, 1999), p. 83.

2. Elaine Dundy, *Elvis and Gladys* (New York: Dell Publishing, 1985), p. 287.

3. Guralnick and Jorgensen, p. 95.

4. Peter Guralnick, *Last Train to Memphis* (Boston: Little, Brown, 1994), p. 399.

5. Ibid., p. 397

6. Jerry Hopkins, *Elvis* (New York: Simon and Schuster, 1971), p. 189.

7. Ibid., p. 163

Chapter Eight. Military Man

1. Peter Guralnick and Ernst Jorgensen, *Elvis Day by Day* (New York : Ballantine Books, 1999), p. 120.

2. Peter Guralnick, *Last Train to Memphis* (Boston: Little, Brown, 1994), p. 461.

3. Jerry Hopkins, *Elvis* (New York: Simon and Schuster, 1971), p. 205.

4. Guralnick and Jorgensen, p. 120.

5. Albert Goldman, *Elvis* (New York: McGraw-Hill, 1981), pp. 278–279.

6. Rose Clayton and Dick Heard, *Elvis Up Close* (Atlanta, Georgia: Turner Publishing, 1994), p. 146.

7. Ibid., p. 147.

8. Elaine Dundy, *Elvis and Gladys* (New York: Dell Publishing, 1985), p. 358.

9. Clayton and Heard, p. 148.

10. Hopkins, p. 225.

11. Peter Guralnick, *Careless Love* (Boston: Back Bay Books, 1999), p. 21.

12. Guralnick and Jorgensen, p. 129.

13. Ibid., p. 144.

Chapter Nine. Difficult Days

1. Memphis Press-Scimitar, March 7, 1960.

2. Alanna Nash, *Elvis Aaron Presley: Revelations from the Memphis Mafia* (New York: Harper Collins, 1995), p. 173.

3. Ibid., p. 175

4. Peter Guralnick, *Careless Love* (Boston: Back Bay Books, 1999), p. 65.

5. Jerry Hopkins, *Elvis* (New York: Simon & Schuster, 1971), p. 251.

6. Nash, p. 259.

7. Guralnick, p. 77.

8. Rose Clayton and Dick Heard, *Elvis Up Close* (Atlanta, Georgia: Turner Publishing, 1994), p. 176.

9. Nash, p. 205.

10. Guralnick, p. 164.

11. Peter Guralnick and Ernst Jorgensen, *Elvis Day by Day* (New York: Ballantine Books, 1999), p. 198.

12. Guralnick, p. 189.

13. Ibid., p. 244.

14. Cindy Hazen and Mike Freeman, *The Best of Elvis* (Memphis, Tenn.: Memphis Explorations), p. 19.

15. Guralnick, p. 223.

16. Ibid., p. 232.

17. Priscilla Beaulieu Presley, *Elvis and Me* (New York: Berkley Books, 1985), p. 256.

Chapter Ten. Comeback King

1. Priscilla Beaulieu Presley, *Elvis and Me* (New York: Berkley Books, 1985), p. 268.

2. Peter Guralnick and Ernst Jorgensen, *Elvis Day by Day* (New York: Ballantine Books, 1999), p. 255.

3. Peter Guralnick, *Careless Love* (Boston: Back Bay Books, 1999), p. 368.

4. Ibid., p. 351.

5. Ibid., p. 348.

6. Alanna Nash, *Elvis Aaron Presley: Revelations from the Memphis Mafia* (New York: Harper Collins, 1995), p. 660.

7. Cindy Hazen and Mike Freeman, *The Best of Elvis* (Memphis, Tenn.: Memphis Explorations), p. 10.

8. Guralnick and Jorgensen, p. 300.

9. Nash, p. 536.

10. Presley, p. 276.

11. Nash, p. 532.

Chapter Eleven. Perplexing Performer

1. Peter Guralnick and Ernst Jorgensen, *Elvis Day by Day* (New York: Ballantine Books, 1999), p. 327.

2. Peter Guralnick, *Careless Love* (Boston: Back Bay Books, 1999), p. 551.

3. Guralnick and Jorgensen, p. 355.

4. Laura Levin and John O'Hara, *Elvis & You* (New York: Berkley Publishing Group, 2000), p. 584.

5. Guralnick and Jorgensen, p. 363.

6. Ibid., p. 361.

7. Guralnick, p. 649.

8. Ibid., p. 651.

9. Author interview with Bernard Lansky, August 2001.

10. Guralnick, p. 658.

Chapter Twelve. Elvis Presley's Legacy

1. Dirk Vellenga, *Elvis and the Colonel* (New York: Delacorte Press, 1988), p. 176.

2. Lorraine Redd and Jack E. Davis, *Only in Mississippi* (Brandon, Miss: Quail Ridge Press, 1993), p. 13.

3. "Elvis Is Alive," *Weekly World News*, May 27, 2003, pp. 1, 2.

4. Lee Frydman, "Elvis Autopsy Report" at <http://www.elvispresleynews.com> (August 2001).

5. Chris Davidson, "Elvis, an American Legend," (Beverly Hills, Calif.: L.F.P. Publishing, 1995), p. 55.

6. Alanna Nash, *Elvis Aaron Presley, Revelations from the Memphis Mafia* (New York: HarperCollins, 1995), p 763.

7. Jerry Hopkins, *Elvis* (New York: Simon & Schuster, 1971), p. 42.

Further Reading

Alagna, Magdalena. *Elvis Presley.* New York: Rosen, 2002.

Brown, Adele. *Elvis Presley.* Milwaukee, Wisc.: World Almanac Library, 2003.

Daily, Robert. *Elvis Presley, The King of Rock 'n' Roll.* New York: Franklin Watts, 2000.

Denenberg, Barry. *All Shook Up: The Life and Death of Elvis Presley.* New York: Scholastic, 2003.

Frew, Tim. *Elvis: A Life in Pictures.* New York: Barnes and Noble, Inc., 1997.

Mason, Bobbie Ann. *Elvis Presley.* New York: Viking, 2003.

Internet Addresses

Official Elvis Web Site
<http://www.elvis.com>

The "Unofficial" Elvis Home Page
<http://www.ibiblio.org/elvis/elvishom.html>

Biography with Lots of Photos
<http://www.history-of-rock.com/elvis_presley.htm>

Index

Page numbers for photographs are in **boldface** type.